Harold R. Foster

Prince Valiant

COMPRISING PAGES 1281 THROUGH 1326

Monastery Of The Demons

FANTAGRAPHICS BOOKS

ABOUT THIS EDITION:

Produced in cooperation with the Danish publisher Interpresse and several other publishers around the world, this new edition of *PRINCE VALIANT* is intended to be the definitive compilation of Hal Foster's masterpiece.

Although "Monastery Of The Demons" is billed as "Volume 29," this is in fact only the fourth American release in a new series of *PRINCE VALIANT* books. Future releases (Vol. 30 through Vol. 40) are planned to follow sequentially, reprinting the strip until Foster's last work on it in the early '70s. The volumes will be released at the rate of two or three a year, with hopes of eventually graduating to a quarterly schedule.

Additionally, Interpresse and Fantagraphics Books intend to publish the first 25 volumes (comprising Foster's first 22 years on the strip) as an ongoing, "parallel" series, with the ultimate goal of having 40 volumes in print, reprinting the complete *PRINCE VALIANT* by Hal Foster.

ABOUT THE PUBLISHER:

Celebrating its 10th anniversary in 1986, FANTAGRAPHICS BOOKS has dedicated itself to bringing readers the finest in comic book and comic strip material, both new and old. Its "classics" division includes the eight-volume *The Complete E.C. Segar Popeye* and the monthly *NEMO: The Classic Comics Library*. Its "modern" division is responsible for such works as Yellow Kid Award-winner *Love and Rockets* by Los Bros. Hernandez, Peter Bagge's *Neat Stuff*, and the science-fiction color comic *Dalgoda*. See the back cover for a complete listing.

PREVIOUS VOLUMES IN THIS SERIES:

PRINCE VALIANT, Volume 29
"Monastery of the Demons"
comprising pages 1281 (August 27, 1961) through 1326 (July 8, 1962)
Published by Fantagraphics Books, 4359 Cornell Road, Agoura, CA 91301
Editorial Co-Ordinator: Henning Kure
Colored by Camillo Conti
Cover inked by Gorm Transgaard and colored by Søren Håkansson
Fantagraphics Books staff: Kim Thompson & Tom Mason
Copyright © 1986 King Features Syndicate, Inc., Bull's, Interpresse, and Fantagraphics Books, Inc.
Printed in Belgium
ISBN 0-930193-19-9
First printing: Spring, 1986

Prince Valiant
IN THE DAYS OF KING ARTHUR
WRITTEN AND ILLUSTRATED BY HAROLD R FOSTER

Our Story: NICILOS, PRINCE VALIANT'S SHREWD BUSINESS MANAGER, RETURNS FROM THE CITY, HURRIEDLY. HE HAD WON AT THE GAMING TABLE, BUT HIS METHODS WERE QUESTIONED AND HE DARE NOT GO BACK.

HE MUST FIND SOME AMUSEMENT CLOSER AT HAND. THEN HIS EYES FALL UPON TALOON. WHY HAD HE NOT NOTICED HER SAVAGE BEAUTY BEFORE?

HE REGARDS WOMEN AS BRIGHTLY COLORED PLAYTHINGS FOR HIS ENTERTAINMENT. BUT THIS ONE CANNOT UNDERSTAND HIS WIT AND CLEVER SAYINGS. INSTEAD SHE READS HIS INTENTIONS AND HER EYES BLAZE IN ANGER.

TO NICILOS THIS REBUFF IS A CHALLENGE; HE DESIRES MOST WHAT IS DENIED HIM. WHAT HAD BEGUN AS A FLIRTATION NOW BECOMES A BURNING DESIRE. THAT HIS FRIEND OHMED CONFESSES HIS LOVE FOR THE GIRL MAKES NOT AN OUNCE OF DIFFERENCE, FOR HIS CODE IS: 'GET WHAT YOU WANT!'

VAL, EVER-COURTEOUS AND KIND, IS SO PREOCCUPIED WITH THOUGHTS OF RETURNING TO HIS BELOVED ALETA THAT HE DOES NOT NOTICE......

....THAT TALOON HAS GIVEN HIM HER HEART AND WILL FOLLOW HIM AS LONG AS LIFE LASTS, AS HIS SLAVE IF NEED BE.

AND OHMED, AFTER TEN YEARS OF SLAVERY, IS FREE TO TAKE A WIFE. TALOON IS HIS DREAM OF PARADISE.

BUT NICILOS ALSO DESIRES HER AND WILL USE ALL HIS TRICKS, FAIR OR FOUL, TO GET HIS ENDS.

HOW THE FATES MUST HAVE LAUGHED AS THEY WOVE THE THREADS OF FOUR LIVES INTO THIS TRAGIC MESS. FOR NICILOS IS SHARPENING A DEADLY WEAPON, JEALOUSY!

"SEE HOW OFTEN TALOON VISITS THE TENT OF PRINCE VALIANT! WOULD I WERE A HANDSOME PRINCE SO I COULD COMMAND THE FAVORS OF PRETTY GIRLS."

1281

HAL FOSTER

OHMED KNOWS HIS MASTER TO BE AN HONORABLE MAN, BUT THE SEEDS OF JEALOUSY HAVE BEEN SOWN AND HATRED BEGINS TO BURN IN HIS HEART LIKE A SMALL FLAME.

NEXT WEEK- The Final Treachery

8-27-61

Prince Valiant
IN THE DAYS OF KING ARTHUR
WRITTEN AND ILLUSTRATED BY HAROLD R FOSTER

Our Story : IN THE BEGINNING NICILOS ONLY WANTED TO AMUSE HIMSELF WITH TALOON, BUT NOW A BURNING DESIRE FOR HER HAS BEREFT HIM OF ALL REASON.

SHE WILL NEVER NOTICE HIM AS LONG AS MATTERS STAND AS THEY ARE. TO BRING ABOUT A CHANGE, NO MATTER WHAT, HE NEVER FAILS TO FAN THE FLAME OF OHMED'S JEALOUSY.

PRINCE VALIANT IS OFTEN WITH HER, FOR HE IS ANXIOUS TO HAVE THE HORSES IN CONDITION FOR A SWIFT JOURNEY HOME. HE IS INNOCENT OF THE EMOTIONS THAT ARE BUILDING UP SO TRAGICALLY AROUND HIM.

THE EVENING MEAL OF LAMB AND RICE, EATEN WITH THE FINGERS, USED TO BE A MERRY AFFAIR. NOW, IN SILENCE, OHMED RISES AND WALKS AWAY, HIS FACE WHITE WITH PAIN, FOR HE CANNOT BEAR TO SEE THE LOOK OF ADORATION IN TALOON'S EYES AS SHE LOOKS AT VAL.

NICILOS ENTERS THEIR TENT, AND THERE IS OHMED SHARPENING HIS DAGGER!

"SO!" HE SNEERS, "THE SLAVE HAS AT LAST BECOME A MAN. MAY YOUR COURAGE HOLD UNTIL YOU HAVE DEFENDED THE WOMAN YOU LOVE. MAY ALL THE GODS LEND STRENGTH TO YOUR ARM!"

THIS NIGHT, ONE, OR PERHAPS TWO OF HIS RIVALS WILL BE REMOVED, HIS BEST FRIEND OR A KINDLY MASTER. HE IS SICK WITH REMORSE AT HIS OWN TREACHERY. BUT HE DOES NOTHING.
NEXT WEEK- The Fateful Night

1282.

9-3-61

Prince Valiant
IN THE DAYS OF KING ARTHUR
WRITTEN AND ILLUSTRATED BY HAROLD R FOSTER

Our Story: OHMED TAKES HIS SHARPENED KNIFE OUT INTO THE NIGHT AND WALKS TOWARD PRINCE VALIANT'S TENT. OH, HOW CLEVER IS THE GLIB TONGUE OF NICILOS! IT HAS TURNED THIS GENTLE YOUTH INTO A KILLER.

VAL AND ARN ARE PREPARING TO RETIRE WHEN HE ENTERS. HE WALKS BEHIND THE FRIEND WHO HAS FREED HIM FROM SLAVERY AND DRAWS HIS KNIFE.

AT ARN'S WARNING SHOUT VAL SWINGS ASIDE, BUT THE KNIFE IS SWIFTER AND PAIN COMES LIKE A SEARING FLAME.

BEFORE ARN CAN REACH HIS SWORD TALOON BURSTS INTO THE TENT. A GLANCE SHOWS HER THE STAINED KNIFE IN OHMED'S HAND AND ON THE GROUND THE MAN SHE SO ARDENTLY BUT HOPELESSLY LOVES.

HIS RAGE HAS SPENT ITSELF. HE STANDS AS ONE IN A DREAM. LOOKING INTO THE GIRL'S TRAGIC FACE, HE CAN CLEARLY SEE THAT HIS MAD DEED WILL BREAK HER HEART AND THAT HIS DREAMS OF A PARADISE ON EARTH ARE AT AN END. MOTIONLESS HE AWAITS HER THRUST.

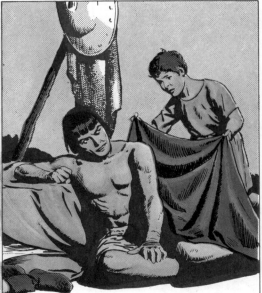

ARN KNEELS BESIDE HIS FATHER AND EXAMINES THE WOUND. "IS IT BAD, SON?" ASKS VAL. "AWFUL, SIRE, WE MUST HAVE HELP."

1283

HAL FOSTER

NICILOS PEERS FROM HIS TENT. HIS TREACHERY HAS REMOVED ALL RIVALS, BUT HOOFBEATS FADING INTO THE NIGHT INDICATE THE PRIZE IS GONE.

NEXT WEEK—A Persian Garden

9-10-61

Prince Valiant
IN THE DAYS OF KING ARTHUR
WRITTEN AND ILLUSTRATED BY HAROLD R FOSTER

Our Story : FROM HIS TENT NICILOS WATCHES THE AWFUL RESULTS OF HIS SCHEMING. A MAGI TAKES THE BODY OF POOR OHMED TO THE TEMPLE OF ZOROASTER FOR FUNERAL SERVICES.....

.....WHILE A PALANQUIN BEARS THE WOUNDED PRINCE VALIANT TO THE HOME OF A WEALTHY MERCHANT.

THE WAY LEADS THROUGH NOISOME ALLEYS, CROWDED AND STIFLING.

BUT A DOORWAY OPENS INTO A COURTYARD WHERE FOUNTAINS PLAY AND FLOWERS BLOOM. THEIR HOST WELCOMES THEM AND SENDS FOR HIS OWN PHYSICIAN TO HEAL VAL'S WOUND.

"A VERY CLUMSY PIECE OF WORK," MUTTERS THE HEALER. "YOUR ASSAILANT WAS A VERY POOR CRAFTSMAN. SEE, HE HELD THE BLADE THUS, AND IT COULD NOT GO BETWEEN YOUR RIBS," AND HE SHAKES HIS HEAD SADLY AT SUCH A SHODDY PERFORMANCE.

NOW NICILOS IS LEFT ALONE IN CHARGE OF THE CARAVAN AND IS IN A POSITION TO ROB HIS MASTER OF ALL HIS GOODS. SUCH AN OPPORTUNITY MIGHT NOT COME HIS WAY AGAIN.

1264.

BUT HE HESITATES. FAR OUT IN THE DESERT TALOON IS RIDING HOMEWARD TO HER DOOM.

9-17-61

TO HIS OWN ASTONISHMENT HE FINDS HE WANTS THE GIRL MORE THAN RICHES! HE STEALS BUT TWO HORSES AND RIDES IN PURSUIT.
NEXT WEEK-**The Meeting**

Prince Valiant

IN THE DAYS OF KING ARTHUR

WRITTEN AND ILLUSTRATED BY HAROLD R FOSTER

Our Story: IN A PLEASANT GARDEN IN BAGDAD PRINCE VALIANT RECOVERS FROM A KNIFE WOUND AND ARN IS NOW IN CHARGE OF THE CARAVAN. FROM THE GOSSIP OF THE DROVERS THE STORY OF THE TRAGIC HAPPENINGS OF THE PAST WEEK ARE PIECED TOGETHER.

AS A WOUNDED ANIMAL STRIVES TO REACH ITS LAIR, SO TALOON RIDES EASTWARD TOWARD THE WINDY STEPPES OF HER HOMELAND. SHE WOULD RATHER FACE THE DEATH SENTENCE THAT AWAITS HER THERE THAN LIVE IN THIS LAND.

AND NICILOS FOLLOWS, DRAWN ONWARD BY THE FIRST UNSELFISH LOVE HE HAS EVER KNOWN. HER TRAIL IS EASY TO FOLLOW, FOR AN UNVEILED WOMAN, RIDING ALONE, IS WORTHY OF NOTE.

NO HORSEMAN COULD OVERTAKE THE NIMBLE RIDER, BUT SHE MUST PAUSE OFTEN TO HUNT, AND AT NIGHT DESCEND TO THE VALLEYS TO RAID FIELD AND ORCHARD FOR FRUIT AND MELONS.

ON A MOUNTAIN PASS THEY MEET. "PRINCE VALIANT STILL LIVES," SAYS NICILOS AND WATCHES THE LOOK OF SORROW IN HER EYES TURN INTO RELIEF. "AND I LOVE YOU," HE ADDS.

AND CLEVER NICILOS, ONCE SO SLY AND GLIB, FINDS NO WORDS TO SAY AS HE LOOKS LONGINGLY AT THE PROUD, SELF-RELIANT GIRL BEFORE HIM.

TALOON RETURNS HIS GAZE. THEN THE CLOUDS SWEEP DOWN THE PASS AND THEY ARE OBSCURED IN MIST SO THAT NO ONE KNOWS HOW THEIR STORY ENDS.

NEXT WEEK—**Belchad Abu**

1285.

9-24-61

Prince Valiant
IN THE DAYS OF KING ARTHUR
WRITTEN AND ILLUSTRATED BY HAROLD R FOSTER

Our Story : SOON PRINCE VALIANT'S KNIFE WOUND BECOMES JUST ANOTHER SCAR AMONG THE MANY, AND HE BEGINS PLANNING THEIR HOMEWARD JOURNEY.

PLODDING HORSES ARE EXCHANGED FOR THE SWIFT CAMELS. VAL SIGHS WITH RELIEF WHEN ALL IS READY, FOR NOW THERE WILL BE NO MORE TEDIOUS BICKERING WITH SHREWD MERCHANTS.

ARN HAS HIS FIRST CAMEL RIDE AND LEARNS WHY THE ANIMAL IS CALLED THE 'SHIP OF THE DESERT'. HE BECOMES VIOLENTLY SEASICK!

THEIR CARAVAN IS LEFT FAR BEHIND AS THEY RIDE SWIFTLY UP THE EUPHRATES. AFTER SEVERAL DAYS THEY COME TO THE TOWN OF DEIR EZ ZOR, AND VAL REMEMBERS THIS PLACE ONLY TOO WELL.

"MY SON, DO YOU SEE YONDER FAT MERCHANT? THAT IS BELCHAD ABU. ONCE HE WORE THE 'SINGING SWORD' AND OWNED A SLAVE NAMED PRINCE VALIANT. WE WILL HAVE SOME FUN!"

AND SO THEY ARM THEMSELVES AND FOLLOW. AMONG ITS ORCHARDS AND GARDENS STANDS THE MERCHANT'S VILLA WHERE VAL HAD ONCE FELT THE STING OF THE LASH.

"WE FIND THE CARAVANSARY UNFIT TO ENTERTAIN ROYALTY, SO CRAVE YOUR HOSPITALITY FOR THE NIGHT." THE HAUGHTY MERCHANT LOOKS DISPLEASED WITH THIS INTRUSION UNTIL HIS EYE FALLS ON THE 'SINGING SWORD'. HE TAKES ANOTHER LOOK AT ITS OWNER AND HIS FACE GOES WHITE.

NEXT WEEK- Out of the Past

1286.

10-1-61

Prince Valiant

IN THE DAYS OF KING ARTHUR

WRITTEN AND ILLUSTRATED BY HAROLD R FOSTER

"I AM PRINCE VALIANT, KNIGHT OF ARTHUR'S ROUND TABLE, HEIR TO THE KINGDOM OF THULE. WHEN, IN MY DISTANT HOMELAND, I HEARD TROUBADOURS TELL OF YOUR GREAT LOVELINESS, I TOOK SWORD AND SHIELD AND FOUGHT MY WAY 'ACROSS A THOUSAND LEAGUES OF HOSTILE LAND TO WIN TO YOUR SIDE!"

Our Story: BELCHAD ABU LOOKS INTO THE GRINNING FACE OF HIS ONE-TIME SLAVE AND FEAR SHAKES HIM LIKE A LEAF. DOES THIS NOBLE PRINCE COME HERE TO SEEK REVENGE?

FOR WELL HE REMEMBERS THAT DAY IN DAMASCUS WHEN HE PURCHASED THE GREAT SWORD AND ITS OWNER FROM AN ARAB SLAVE DEALER.

AND HOW THAT YOUNG SLAVE HAD RISKED DEATH BY ENTERING THE WOMEN'S QUARTERS AND MAKING SUCH ROMANTIC LOVE TO HIS DAUGHTER BERNICE THAT SHE HAD HELPED HIM ESCAPE.

SO VAL AND ARN TAKE THEIR EASE AND ENJOY THE DISCOMFITURE OF THEIR TREMBLING HOST. HIS GUEST HAS NO REASON TO LOVE HIM. HE ALSO HAS A BAD HABIT OF FONDLING HIS GLEAMING SWORD HILT. IT'S FRIGHTENING!

BERNICE HAS NEVER FORGOTTEN THE GALLANT LAD WHO HAD MADE LOVE TO HER SO LONG AGO. HE HAD BROKEN HER HEART THOUGH HE HAD NOT DESTROYED HER APPETITE. AND NOW SHE LEARNS HE HAS RETURNED.

"YOU HAVE COME BACK FOR ME," SHE PIPES. "I KNEW MY BEAUTY WOULD HAUNT YOU UNTIL YOU RETURNED." "HOLD!" CRIES VAL, "HAVE YOU FORGOTTEN THAT YOU HAD ME WHIPPED?"

"SILLY BOY," SHE COOS, "THAT WAS NOTHING. I ALWAYS HAVE MY SLAVES WHIPPED."

"YOU MUST HAVE BEEN A GAY BLADE IN YOUR YOUTH, SIRE," MUSES ARN. "DOES MOTHER KNOW SHE MARRIED A GREAT LOVER?" "SHUT UP!" ANSWERS VAL.

NEXT WEEK—**Escape**.

1287   10-8-61

Prince Valiant

IN THE DAYS OF KING ARTHUR

WRITTEN AND ILLUSTRATED BY HAROLD R FOSTER

Our Story: BERNICE ARISES EARLY, THEN, DRESSED IN HER BEST AND SOAKED WITH PERFUME SHE PRACTICES SOME IRRESISTIBLE EXPRESSIONS IN HER MIRROR. FINALLY SHE IS READY TO MEET HER BELOVED.

BUT HER BELOVED HAS GONE, STRIDING AWAY IN THE DAWN WITH HIS YOUNG SON TROTTING BEHIND HIM.

PAMPERED AND SPOILED BERNICE HAS ALWAYS BEEN GIVEN WHAT SHE WANTED .....EXCEPT PRINCE VALIANT. AND, ALTHOUGH SHE SCREAMS AND RENDS HER GARMENTS, NONE OFFER TO BRING HIM BACK.

SHE SEEKS COMFORT BY FLINGING HERSELF INTO HER FATHER'S ARMS .....BUT SHE HAS PUT ON WEIGHT SINCE LAST SHE DID THIS. THEN, SO EVERYONE MIGHT SHARE HER SORROW, SHE ORDERS FIVE LASHES APIECE TO THE SLAVES....AND FEELS MUCH BETTER.

PRINCE VALIANT COMES ROARING INTO THE CARAVANSARY AND ORDERS THE CAMEL MEN TO SADDLE THE ANIMALS AND GET MOVING, FAST.

"AND YOU, MY SON, MENTION ONE WORD OF THIS TO YOUR MOTHER, AND I'LL SKIN YOU ALIVE!"
"BUT, SIRE, YOU KNOW WHAT A LOOSE TONGUE I HAVE."

© 1961, King Features Syndicate, Inc., World rights reserved. .

"THOUGH A BRIGHT NEW DAMASCUS BLADE MIGHT BE OF SUCH IMPORTANCE TO ME THAT I WOULD FORGET ALL LESSER TRIFLES."
"A BLACKMAILER!" MUSES VAL APPROVINGLY.

ALONG THE ROUTE THEY MUST TAKE, A REAL BLACKMAILER AWAITS THE DOOM HE HAS TRULY EARNED, AND PRAYS THAT SOME MIRACLE WILL SAVE HIM.

NEXT WEEK- **Alimann 'the cruel'**

1288.   10·15·61

Prince Valiant
IN THE DAYS OF KING ARTHUR
WRITTEN AND ILLUSTRATED BY HAROLD R FOSTER

Our Story: ALIMANN HAS COMMITTED MANY CRIMES THAT WOULD BRING SHAME TO A LESS EVIL MAN, BUT NOW HE HAS GONE TOO FAR. HIS LATEST DEED MIGHT BRING VENGEANCE, SWIFT AND TERRIBLE, OUT OF THE DESERT.

HE HAD BEEN CAREFUL THAT HIS THIEVING RAIDS WERE MADE FAR FROM HOME, BUT, FROM HIS HILL FORT, HE HAD SEEN ALL THE MEN FROM A NEARBY OASIS VILLAGE RIDE TO THE CONCLAVE IN DEIR EZ ZOR.

THE TEMPTATION WAS TOO GREAT AND HE HAD RAIDED THE HELPLESS VILLAGE. AND NOW, AS HE SEES THE DESERT MEN RETURNING, HE WONDERS IF HIS MEN HAVE LEFT ANYONE ALIVE WHO MIGHT BE SNEAKY ENOUGH TO TELL ON HIM.

OH! HOW HE WISHES HE HAD MORE SWORDSMEN WITHIN HIS STRONG-HOLD! AS IF IN ANSWER TO HIS PRAYER A KNIGHT WITH ARMED GUARDS RIDES BY, AND HE SENDS OUT AN INVITATION.

PRINCE VALIANT, ARN AND THEIR CAMEL GUARD ACCEPT ALIMANN'S HOSPITALITY. IF ATTACK COMES DURING THE NIGHT, THE GUESTS WILL ALSO HAVE TO FIGHT FOR THEIR LIVES, AND EVERY SWORD COUNTS.

BEFORE DAWN ALIMANN AWAKES ONE OF VAL'S CAMEL GUARDS. THERE ARE WHISPERED WORDS AND A PURSE OF MONEY CHANGES HANDS.

AS VAL LEAVES EARLY HE IS NOT SURPRISED THAT ALIMANN IS NOT THERE TO BID THEM FARE-WELL, SO HE LEAVES A MESSAGE OF THANKS AND GOES HIS WAY.

1289.

TOWARD EVENING A TROOP OF HORSEMEN OVER-TAKES THEM AND VAL LOOSENS THE 'SINGING SWORD' IN ITS SCABBARD AND TAKES HIS SHIELD.
NEXT WEEK— **The Stowaway**

10-22-61

Prince Valiant

IN THE DAYS OF KING ARTHUR

WRITTEN AND ILLUSTRATED BY HAROLD R FOSTER

Our Story: THE DESERT MEN GALLOP UP AND SURROUND PRINCE VALIANT, ARN AND THE TWO GUARDS. "WE SEARCH FOR 'ALIMANN THE CRUEL'," SAYS THEIR CHIEFTAIN. "WE LEARNED THAT YOU STAYED THE NIGHT WITH HIM."

"WE WERE GUESTS IN THE STRONGHOLD OF ALIMANN LAST NIGHT BUT LEFT EARLY THIS MORNING WITHOUT SEEING OUR HOST. WHY DO YOU SEARCH FOR HIM?"

"WHEN WE RETURNED TO OUR VILLAGE IT WAS IN RUINS. OUR PARENTS, OUR WIVES AND CHILDREN ALL SLAIN, OUR HOMES PLUNDERED. SUCH IS THE WORK OF 'ALIMANN THE CRUEL'."

"AND TO THINK WE ATE AND DRANK WITH SUCH A MONSTER!" EXCLAIMS VAL. "BUT, AS YOU CAN SEE, HE DOES NOT RIDE WITH US."

BUT THAT EVENING WHEN THE BAGGAGE CAMEL IS UNLOADED IT SEEMS THAT ALIMANN DOES RIDE WITH THEM!

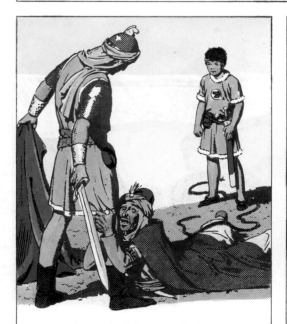

KNIGHTS OF THE ROUND TABLE MUST BE JUDGE, JURY AND EXECUTIONER, IF NEED BE, BUT SHOULD VAL SOIL THE 'SINGING SWORD' ON SUCH CARRION?

ALIMANN BACKS AWAY. IF HE CAN SEIZE THE BOY AS A HOSTAGE....... BUT ARN IS LEARNING HIS TRADE WELL AND IS PREPARED.

THEN HE RUNS. ACROSS THE DARKENING DESERT HE RUNS WITH HIS COMPANION, FEAR!
NEXT WEEK—**Homecoming**

1290.

10-29-61

Prince Valiant
IN THE DAYS OF KING ARTHUR
WRITTEN AND ILLUSTRATED BY HAROLD R FOSTER

Our Story: PRINCE VALIANT WATCHES ALIMANN 'THE CRUEL' RUN, PANIC-STRICKEN, OUT INTO THE DARKENING DESERT AND SHEATHES THE 'SINGING SWORD'.

HOW ARROGANT HE HAD BEEN AS HE RODE THESE SAME PLAINS SURROUNDED BY HIS CUTTHROAT BAND! NOW HE IS ALONE, EVERY MAN AN ENEMY.

WHEN DAY COMES HE HIDES IN A WADI AND, UNDER THE DESERT SUN, LEARNS THE HORRORS OF THIRST.

THE SONS, THE FATHERS AND THE HUSBANDS OF HIS VICTIMS THIRST FOR HIS BLOOD; ONLY WITHIN HIS STRONGHOLD CAN HE HOPE FOR SAFETY.

AT LAST! HE KNOCKS ON THE GATE: "OPEN", HE WHISPERS, "IT IS I, ALIMANN!"

THE GATES OPEN AND HE RUNS TOWARD HIS LIGHTED HALL, SCREAMING ORDERS TO THE SHADOWY FIGURES TO REDOUBLE THEIR WATCH.

HAL FOSTER

ALIMANN, THE CRUEL, AT LAST COMES HOME. AND THERE WAITING FOR HIM ARE THOSE HE FEARS MOST, THE DESERT TRIBE WHOSE VILLAGE HE HAD SO TERRIBLY RAVISHED!

NEXT WEEK - **Sound and Fury**

11-5-61

Prince Valiant

IN THE DAYS OF KING ARTHUR

WRITTEN AND ILLUSTRATED BY HAROLD R. FOSTER

Our Story: FOR WEEKS PRINCE VALIANT HAS FOLLOWED THE BANKS OF THE EUPHRATES, BUT NOW THEY LEAVE THE RIVER AND CROSS OVER THE BARREN HEIGHT OF LAND.

THEN DOWN INTO THE GREEN VALLEY AND ALEPPO, WHERE THE CARAVAN ROUTES CONVERGE. AND VAL HASTENS TO COLLECT THE LETTERS THAT AWAIT HIM THERE.

ALETA WRITES THAT HIS VENTURE INTO TRADE HAS BEEN A GREAT SUCCESS; THAT HER SHIPS ARE CARRYING AN INCREASING AMOUNT OF TRADE GOODS AND THAT HE MUST HURRY HOME. IN FACT, BOLTAR IS EVEN NOW AWAITING HIM IN THE HARBOR OF ANTIOCH.

EAGER AS A SCHOOLBOY VAL RACES TO ANTIOCH TO FIND BOLTAR. THIS IS EASY, AS THE ROAR OF HIS VOICE CAN BE HEARD ABOVE THE TUMULT OF THE BUSY PORT.

BOLTAR, HIS GREAT AXE IN HAND, IS DARING THE HARBOR GUARD TO TRY TO ARREST HIM OR HIS MEN.

VAL RIDES ALONG THE EDGE OF THE QUAY UNTIL EVEN WITH BOLTAR'S SHIP. THEN HE BECKONS THE SAILORS TO LOAD THEIR GEAR WHILE HE PAYS OFF THE CAMEL MEN.

BOLTAR COMES ABOARD GRUMBLING LIKE AN ANGRY VOLCANO. *"THE MANGY, FLEA-BITTEN MERCHANTS OF THIS TOWN WILL GET NO MORE OF MY TRADE!"*

1292.

"I LET MY LADS GO ASHORE FOR A FROLIC. YOU KNOW BOYS WILL BE BOYS. NOW THE UNCOUTH SHOPKEEPERS WANT ME TO PAY DAMAGES!" AND HE SHAKES HIS HEAD AT THE INJUSTICE OF IT ALL.

NEXT WEEK— **The Queen**

HAL FOSTER

11·12·61

Prince Valiant
IN THE DAYS OF KING ARTHUR

WRITTEN AND ILLUSTRATED BY HAROLD R FOSTER

Our Story: ALETA, QUEEN OF THE MISTY ISLES, HAS SENT BOLTAR TO BRING PRINCE VALIANT AND ARN OUT OF THE NEAR EAST AND IT IS QUITE EVIDENT THAT THE SLEEK DRAGONSHIP HAS SAILED THESE WATERS BEFORE. MERCHANT SHIPS SCUTTLE FOR THE SAFETY OF THE NEAREST PORT WHERE SPEARMEN HASTILY MAN THE BATTLEMENTS.

"DID YOU EVER SEE SUCH SUSPICIOUS PEOPLE?" GRUMBLES BOLTAR. "THEIR LACK OF TRUST GIVES ME THAT UNWANTED FEELING."

ONCE AGAIN VAL RETURNS TO A CHANGED WIFE, MORE MATURE NOW, POISED AND SERENE. HOW DIFFERENT FROM THE YOUNG QUEEN WHO HAD LOST A SLIPPER IN A WILD RUSH TO FLING HERSELF INTO HIS ARMS! SHE COMES TO MEET HIM SLOWLY AS IF TO PROLONG THE JOY OF GREETING.

SHE IS, IF POSSIBLE, LOVELIER THAN EVER. HIS EYES ARE BIG WITH WONDER, HIS HANDS TREMBLE AND HE FINDS NO WORDS TO SAY. ALETA SMILES CONTENTEDLY, THE DEAR BOY HAS NOT CHANGED A BIT!

HOW CAN A MAN EVER LEARN TO UNDERSTAND A WOMAN WHO KEEPS CHANGING ALL THE TIME? IT IS NOT RECORDED THAT HE EVER FOUND AN ANSWER TO THE QUESTION.

1295.

AT LAST PRINCE ARN HAS AN AUDIENCE TO LISTEN TO HIS TALES OF ADVENTURE AND THE WONDERS HE HAS SEEN. AND VAL SPENDS JOYOUS HOURS WITH HIS FAMILY, HOURS THAT ARE DOUBLY PRECIOUS FOR THEY COME ALL TOO SELDOM IN THE LIFE OF A PRACTICING WARRIOR.

NEXT WEEK- A Royal Error

11-19-61

Prince Valiant
IN THE DAYS OF KING ARTHUR
WRITTEN AND ILLUSTRATED BY HAROLD R FOSTER

Our Story: PRINCE VALIANT WATCHES HIS WIFE IN AMAZEMENT. WHO WOULD THINK THAT SUCH A PRETTY LITTLE HEAD COULD CONTAIN SUCH MATURE WISDOM? SHE HAS BECOME TRULY A QUEEN WHOSE AUTHORITY IS UNQUESTIONED.

EVEN IN THE COUNCIL OF ELDERS, USUALLY LOUD WITH DEBATE, HER POLICIES ARE ACCEPTED, HER COMMANDS CARRIED OUT.

IN FACT, SHE HAS BECOME SO USED TO AUTHORITY THAT SHE GIVES ORDERS TO HER HUSBAND. IN THE BRITTLE SILENCE THAT FOLLOWS SHE REALIZES HER MISTAKE.

SHE QUICKLY SHIFTS TO HER OWN TRIED AND TRUE FORM OF DIPLOMACY AND THE ANGRY GLINT IN VAL'S EYE SOFTENS. ALETA WILL, OF COURSE, GET HER OWN WAY BUT BY A MUCH SWEETER METHOD.

A SHIP COMES TO THE MISTY ISLES BEARING A WOUNDED KNIGHT WHO ASKS TO BE BORNE TO THE PALACE.

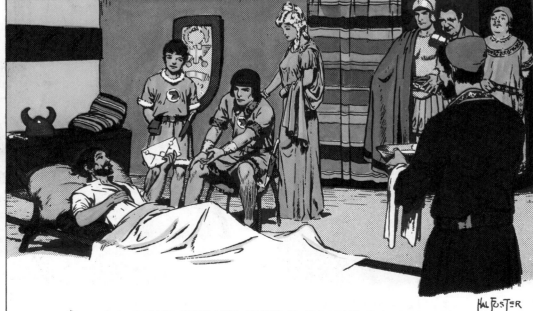

"I BEAR A MESSAGE FROM KING ARTHUR TO PRINCE VALIANT. OF THE FOUR KNIGHTS IN OUR PARTY ONLY I SURVIVED THE JOURNEY THROUGH GAUL."

NEXT WEEK- **The Courier**

HAL FOSTER

1294.

11-26-61

Prince Valiant

IN THE DAYS OF KING ARTHUR

WRITTEN AND ILLUSTRATED BY Harold R Foster

Our Story: KING ARTHUR CALLED FOUR KNIGHTS BEFORE HIM AND SAID: "CARRY THIS MESSAGE TO PRINCE VALIANT IN THE MISTY ISLES. I SEND FOUR OF YOU AS THE WAY ACROSS GAUL IS PERILOUS AND ONE OF YOU MUST GET THROUGH."

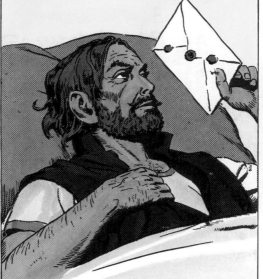

ONLY SIR GOSFORTH SURVIVED AND HE SORELY WOUNDED. FROM HIS BREAST HE TAKES A LETTER AND HANDS IT TO PRINCE VALIANT.

"YOU, SIR VALIANT, ARE BEST EQUIPPED TO BE OUR AMBASSADOR TO ROME", WROTE ARTHUR. "GO TO THEIR EMPEROR IN HIS PALACE AND BESEECH HIS HELP IN OPENING THE ROAD THROUGH GAUL, ELSE CHRISTIAN BRITAIN BE CUT OFF FROM THE REST OF CHRISTENDOM."

"WHEN I HAVE FINISHED MY MISSION TO ROME I MUST RETURN TO CAMELOT TO REPORT MY SUCCESS... OR FAILURE." ALETA SMILES: "I HAVE ALREADY PREPARED MY GOVERNMENT TO FUNCTION IN MY ABSENCE, FOR I GO WITH YOU."

"AND IT WILL BE A GREAT BUSINESS VENTURE, FOR WE WILL GO IN A FLEET OF SHIPS LOADED WITH GOODS, AND TRADE FOR TIN, FURS, AMBER AND GOLD. IF GAUL IS CLOSED, WE WILL OPEN A SEA ROUTE!"

VAL AND ARN DEPART IN BOLTAR'S LONG-SHIP TO COMPLETE HIS MISSION AND RENDEZVOUS WITH THE FLEET AT GIBRALTAR.

QUEEN ALETA LEAVES HER HAPPY LITTLE KINGDOM. IN HER SHORT STAY STRONG WALLS HAVE BEEN BUILT, AN INVASION CRUSHED, AND A CAPTURED FLEET IS BRINGING IN RICHES.
THE MISTY ISLES FADE INTO THE DISTANCE AND SHE IS NO LONGER A QUEEN, ONLY MADAM VALIANT, BUT SHE IS CONTENT.
NEXT WEEK—**Rome**

HAL FOSTER

12-3-61

Prince Valiant
IN THE DAYS OF KING ARTHUR

WRITTEN AND
ILLUSTRATED BY HAROLD R FOSTER

Our Story: BOLTAR'S SHIP LANDS AT OSTIA AND PRINCE VALIANT AND ARN TAKE THE ROAD TO ROME. THEY RIDE BY FIELDS CHOKED WITH WEEDS, RUINED VILLAS; EVEN THE TOMBS OF FAMOUS GENERALS ARE LOOTED AND DEFACED. THE FEW PEOPLE THEY MEET ARE IN RAGS.

AS THEY ENTER THE GATES ARN GASPS: "THE TEMPLES AND PALACES OF ROME MAKE HER THE QUEEN CITY OF THE WORLD!" THEN HE ADDS, "BUT THE BEGGARS OF BAGDAD WERE BETTER CLOTHED THAN ROMAN CITIZENS!"

THEN THEY FIND LODGINGS IN A PALACE. SO OFTEN HAS IT BEEN PILLAGED THAT ITS PATRICIAN OWNER IS GLAD TO TAKE IN PAYING GUESTS.

NOW BEGINS VAL'S EFFORT TO SEE THE EMPEROR. ONLY WITH BRIBES CAN HE GET FROM DOORMAN UP TO CHAMBERLAIN. IT WILL COST A FORTUNE TO REACH HIS GOAL.

VAL IS NOT USED TO THESE MEAN WAYS. HE FEELS DEGRADED AND TELLS OF HIS DISAPPOINTMENT TO HIS GENTLE HOST.

"I STILL RETAIN SOCIAL POSITION AND SOME SMALL INFLUENCE AND COULD INVITE GUESTS HIGH IN GOVERNMENT TO A BANQUET." HE HOLDS HIS HEAD PROUDLY TO OVERCOME HIS SHAME AS HE ADDS, "YOU WILL HAVE TO PAY THE COST, I CAN NO LONGER AFFORD IT."

ROME IS LIKE A BEAUTIFUL LADY WHO, GROWN CARELESS IN HER WAYS, WITH DIRTY FACE AND TORN GARMENTS, AWAITS FURTHER MISFORTUNE.
NEXT WEEK- **The Ruined Queen**

HAL FOSTER

1296.

12-10-61

Prince Valiant
IN THE DAYS OF KING ARTHUR
WRITTEN AND ILLUSTRATED BY HAROLD R FOSTER

Our Story: PRINCE VALIANT AND HIS HOST ARRANGE A BANQUET SO THAT VAL MAY MEET SOME INFLUENTIAL MEN IN GOVERNMENT AND THROUGH THEM GET AN AUDIENCE WITH THE EMPEROR.

THE STREETS OF ROME TELL ARN A SAD STORY. POVERTY IS THE LOT OF ITS PEOPLE, AND GROUPS OF BARBARIANS WANDER ABOUT AT WILL SEEKING PLEASURE.

TWO GRACEFUL PILLARS OF MARBLE, INTRICATELY CARVED, STAND BEFORE A RUINED PALACE. WITH GREAT SHOUTING AND LAUGHTER THE GOTHS ARE HEAVING ON ROPES FLUNG OVER THE TOP.

AT LAST THE SLENDER COLUMNS TOPPLE AND, WITH A THUNDEROUS ROAR, ARE REDUCED TO RUBBLE. AT THIS THE BARBARIANS SHRIEK WITH DELIGHT FOR, UNABLE TO CREATE BEAUTY THEMSELVES, THEY TAKE JOY IN ITS DESTRUCTION!

BEYOND A GARDEN WALL A SMALL SWEET VOICE IS SINGING. ONLY A VERY BEAUTIFUL GARDEN COULD INSPIRE SUCH A HAPPY SONG AND ARN WOULD LIKE TO SEE IT. HE CAN, IN FACT, FOR THE WINDOW OF A RUINED BUILDING OVERLOOKS THE GARDEN.

BUT HERE IS A MYSTERY. THERE IS CERTAINLY A WINDOW ON THE OUTSIDE, BUT NONE INSIDE! OR COULD THERE BE A SECRET PASSAGE?

HE CLIMBS TO THE TOP, AND THERE, SURE ENOUGH, IS A STAIRWAY WITHIN THE THICKNESS OF THE WALL AND A WINDOW.

1297.

HAL FOSTER

THE FOLIAGE IS SO HIGH HE CAN ONLY SEE THE TOP OF A MARBLE PAVILION. THE STAIRS CONTINUE DOWNWARD AND A FAINT GLEAM OF LIGHT MAY MEAN A DOORWAY.

NEXT WEEK - The Enchanted Garden

12-17-61

Prince Valiant
IN THE DAYS OF KING ARTHUR
WRITTEN AND ILLUSTRATED BY HAROLD R FOSTER

Our Story : PRINCE ARN DESCENDS THE SECRET STAIRWAY CAREFULLY, THE WOODEN DOOR AT THE BOTTOM CRUMBLES IN HIS HAND AND A KICK BREAKS THE RUSTED LOCK ON THE IRON GRILL. THEN HE IS IN THE GARDEN.

A WILDERNESS OF WEEDS AND BRAMBLES GREETS HIM, BUT A PAVED WALK CREATES A TUNNEL THROUGH WHICH HE CRAWLS.

ARN EMERGES INTO A WELL-KEPT GARDEN, BRIGHT WITH FLOWERS. "I HEARD YOU COMING," CALLS A VOICE, "ARE YOU A PRINCE ?"

"YES, I AM PRINCE ARN."
"AND DO YOU RIDE A WHITE HORSE ?" SHE ASKS.
"YES, I HAVE A WHITE HORSE AT CAMELOT."
"THEN YOU HAVE COME TO RESCUE ME FROM OUT OF THIS ENCHANTED GARDEN!"

"FOR ONLY A PRINCE ON A WHITE HORSE CAN BREAK THE SPELL OF THE EVIL SORCERESS WHO KEEPS ME IMPRISONED." WHAT A STRANGE LITTLE ELF THIS IS, THINKS ARN, NOT ONCE HAS SHE LOOKED AT ME.

"SO, YESTERDAY I WAS A GOOD FAIRY; TODAY I AM AN EVIL WITCH! WELL, FOR NOW I AM JUST YOUR OLD NANA AND HAVE LAID OUT YOUR LUNCH."

1298.

"YOU SEE HOW SHE CHANGES ? IT IS MAGIC," AND THE GIRL REACHES FOR HIM, MISSES, TRIES AGAIN AND CATCHES HIS SLEEVE. "COME ON," SHE SAYS.

ONLY THEN DOES ARN REALIZE THAT SHE IS BLIND. BLIND BUT LIVING IN A BEAUTIFUL WORLD OF FANTASY.
NEXT WEEK—
The World behind the Garden Wall.

HAL FOSTER

12-24-61

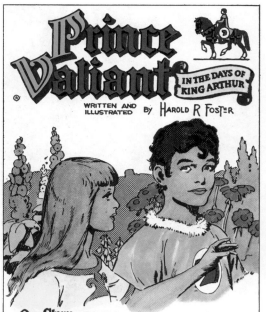

Prince Valiant
IN THE DAYS OF KING ARTHUR
WRITTEN AND ILLUSTRATED BY HAROLD R FOSTER

Our Story ⁑ SEEKING ADVENTURE, PRINCE ARN FOLLOWS A SECRET PASSAGE AND COMES TO AN ENCHANTED GARDEN. HERE A BLIND PRINCESS IS WAITING TO BE RESCUED FROM A WITCH. BUT THE WITCH CALLS THEM TO LUNCH, SO THE ESCAPE IS POSTPONED.

SHE LEADS ARN BY THE HAND. *"THE PATH IS HERE,"* SHE INSTRUCTS, *"NOW WE COME TO THREE STEPS, NOW THE PATH TURNS....."* ARN HAS THE STRANGE FEELING THAT HE IS ACTUALLY LIVING IN A FAIRY TALE.

THEN HE MAKES A DISCOVERY. NOT ONLY IS THE SMALL MISS BLIND, BUT SHE HAS NEVER BEEN TOLD THAT OTHERS CAN SEE!

"MY MOTHER IS COMING, SHE IS VERY BEAUTIFUL," ANNOUNCES THE PRINCESS, *"AND THUMP, THUMP, THUMP, HERE COMES MY FATHER."* THEN SHE WHISPERS: *"I AM REALLY NOT A PRINCESS, BUT I WILL BE WHEN MY FATHER IS EMPEROR."*

"HOW DID THIS BOY GET INTO THE GARDEN AND WHO IS HE?" DEMANDS THE FATHER.

"I AM PRINCE ARN, SON OF SIR VALIANT, AND I CAME BY WAY OF A SECRET PASSAGE AMONG THE BRIARS AT THE FOOT OF THE GARDEN," ANSWERS ARN.

"SIR VALIANT?" MUSES THE FATHER, *"ISN'T HE THE KNIGHT WHO IS TRYING TO GAIN AUDIENCE WITH THE EMPEROR ON BEHALF OF KING ARTHUR OF BRITAIN?"*

1299.

ARN TELLS OF HIS SIRE'S MISSION AND THE DIFFICULTIES HE MEETS IN HIS EFFORT TO REACH THE EMPEROR. ONLY WHEN THE TALE IS TOLD DOES THE BLIND GIRL SPEAK:

12-31-61

"NOW LET THE PRINCE TELL OF HIS TRAVELS TO FABULOUS CATHAY AND THE MAGIC ISLES OF SPICE; OF THE WONDROUS ADVENTURES HE HAS HAD AND THE STRANGE PEOPLE HE HAS MET!"
NEXT WEEK - **The Story Teller**

Prince Valiant
IN THE DAYS OF KING ARTHUR
WRITTEN AND ILLUSTRATED By HAROLD R FOSTER

Our Story: PRINCE ARN DISCOVERS A SECRET PASSAGE AND ENTERS A GARDEN, THE ABODE OF A LITTLE BLIND GIRL, WHO BELIEVES IN FAIRY TALES.

"COME, PRINCE ARN, SHOW ME THIS HIDDEN ENTRANCE," SAYS HER FATHER.

"YES, LAD, I KNOW OF THIS GATE AND I MUST REPAIR IT. I BROUGHT YOU AWAY TO ASK YOU TO GUARD WELL YOUR TONGUE WHEN YOU SPEAK TO MY DAUGHTER."

"FOR HER DAYS ARE NUMBERED AND THEY ARE FEW. WE STRIVE TO MAKE THOSE DAYS HAPPY, AND SO HAVE NOT TOLD HER SHE IS BLIND OR THAT OTHERS ARE MORE FORTUNATE."

THE CHILD'S SIGHTLESS EYES GROW BIG WITH WONDER AS ARN TELLS THE SAGAS OF THE NORSE HEROES. IT IS EASY TO BELIEVE THIS IS AN ENCHANTED GARDEN AND AT ANY MOMENT A FAIRY OR ELF MAY APPEAR.

THE OLD NANA BREAKS THE SPELL: "COME, CHILD, YOU HAVE HAD ENOUGH EXCITEMENT FOR THE DAY AND IT IS TIME FOR YOUR REST."

AS ARN LEAVES THE VILLA THE FATHER STOPS HIM. "YOU HAVE BROUGHT PLEASURE TO MY DAUGHTER. IN GRATITUDE I MIGHT SAVE THE NOBLE SIR VALIANT MUCH TROUBLE. SEND HIM TO ME."

1300.

ARN HASTENS TO THEIR LODGINGS BUT HIS FATHER IS WELCOMING THE GUESTS ARRIVING FOR THE BANQUET, AND HE WILL HAVE TO WITHHOLD THE OFFER UNTIL THE MORROW.

NEXT WEEK- **The Banquet**

HAL FOSTER

1-7-62

Prince Valiant
IN THE DAYS OF KING ARTHUR
WRITTEN AND ILLUSTRATED BY HAROLD R FOSTER

Our Story RETURNS TO PRINCE VALIANT AND HIS EFFORTS TO REACH THE EMPEROR. HIS KINDLY HOST HAS SPREAD A BANQUET AND INVITED AS GUESTS MEN HIGH IN GOVERNMENT IN THE HOPE THEY MIGHT AID VAL IN HIS QUEST.

BUT WHEN VAL MAKES MENTION OF HIS PROJECT THEY ADROITLY TURN THE CONVERSATION. THEY WOULD HELP NO ONE BUT THEMSELVES. THAT THEY HAD HELPED THEMSELVES IS EVIDENT BY THEIR WEALTH.

THE REPARTEE IS WITTY, THE CONVERSATION BRILLIANT, BUT ANY MENTION OF POLITICS IS AVOIDED AS IF IT WERE SOMETHING MENACING THEY WISHED TO FORGET.

WHEN, AT DAWN, THE BANQUET ENDS, VAL KNOWS ONE THING: THAT DESPITE THE GAIETY AND LOUD LAUGHTER THESE MEN DISTRUST AND FEAR EACH OTHER.

"MY PLAN WAS ONLY AN EXPENSIVE FAILURE," SAYS HIS HOST. "I HAVE THE IMPRESSION MY FRIENDS WOULD RATHER PREVENT THAN HELP YOU MEET THE EMPEROR."

ARN OFFERS A RAY OF HOPE. "I MADE FRIENDS WITH A LITTLE BLIND GIRL, AND HER FATHER TOLD ME HE MIGHT BE OF SERVICE TO YOU."

1301.

VAL IS WILLING TO TRY ANYTHING THAT WILL BRING HIS PETITION BEFORE THE EMPEROR, SO HE BIDS ARN LEAD THE WAY.

NEXT WEEK **The Doomed City**

1-14-62

Prince Valiant
IN THE DAYS OF KING ARTHUR
WRITTEN AND ILLUSTRATED BY HAROLD R. FOSTER

Our Story: PRINCE VALIANT FOLLOWS HIS SON TO THE HOME OF MARCUS SEVERIS WHO HAS PROMISED HIM AID. THE LITTLE BLIND GIRL TAKES ARN TO THE GARDEN TO LISTEN TO HIS WONDROUS TALES AND HER FATHER SEATS VAL ON THE PATIO.

"MY MISSION IS SIMPLE. UNLESS THE ROAD THROUGH GAUL IS OPENED, CHRISTIAN BRITAIN WILL BE CUT OFF FROM THE REST OF CHRISTENDOM. KING ARTHUR REQUESTS AID FROM THE EMPEROR OF ROME."

"YOU WILL NEVER DELIVER YOUR PETITION," SAYS MARCUS QUIETLY. "THE EMPEROR IS SURROUNDED BY FAWNING POLITICIANS, EACH SEEKING HIS FAVOR. WHO AMONG THEM WOULD RISK HIS POSITION BY INTRODUCING SO UNPLEASANT A SUBJECT AS AID? ROME CANNOT EVEN PROTECT ITS OWN WALLS!"

"OUR LEGIONS COULD NOT PREVENT THE GOTHS FROM CROSSING THE MIGHTY RHINE. HOW COULD THEY BE EXPECTED TO HOLD A NARROW RIBBON OF ROAD? THE GOTHS HAVE SPREAD OVER EUROPE, OTHER TRIBES FOLLOW AND THIS FORWARD MOVEMENT EXTENDS AS FAR BACK AS THE BALTIC."

"ROME IS DOOMED! WHO WOULD FIGHT FOR HER? THE POPULACE STARVES, THE WEALTH AND POWER IS IN THE HANDS OF A SELFISH FEW. BEYOND OUR BORDERS BARBARIAN CHIEFTAINS ALREADY GAZE OUR WAY."

"MY MISSION THEN IS A FAILURE AND IT IS SAD NEWS I MUST BRING TO MY KING."

1302.

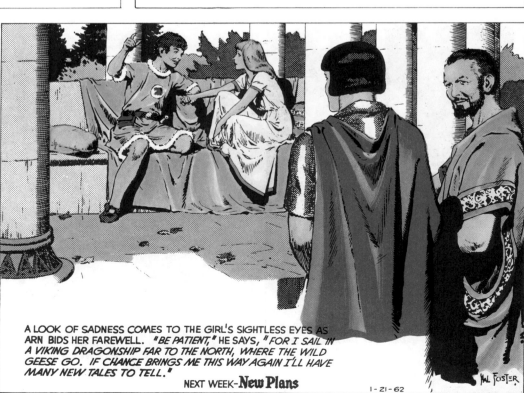

A LOOK OF SADNESS COMES TO THE GIRL'S SIGHTLESS EYES AS ARN BIDS HER FAREWELL. "BE PATIENT," HE SAYS, "FOR I SAIL IN A VIKING DRAGONSHIP FAR TO THE NORTH, WHERE THE WILD GEESE GO. IF CHANCE BRINGS ME THIS WAY AGAIN I'LL HAVE MANY NEW TALES TO TELL."

NEXT WEEK- **New Plans**

1-21-62

HAL FOSTER

Prince Valiant
IN THE DAYS OF KING ARTHUR
WRITTEN AND ILLUSTRATED BY Harold R Foster

Our Story: PRINCE VALIANT RIDES AWAY FROM ROME, HIS MISSION A FAILURE. BUT ARN LOOKS BACK OFTEN TO WHERE THE CITY CROWNS ITS SEVEN HILLS, THE MORNING SUN SHINING ON ITS MARBLE PALACES AND THE SQUALOR AND POVERTY OF ITS STREETS HIDDEN. IT HAD BEEN FORETOLD THAT THE BARBARIANS WOULD ONCE MORE DESTROY IT, BUT WOULD IT DIE AS DID BABYLON, OR RETURN AGAIN AS 'THE ETERNAL CITY'?

ON BOLTAR'S LONGSHIP THEY SAIL TO RENDEZVOUS WITH ALETA'S FLEET. VAL HAS BOUGHT MANY MAPS IN ROME AND THESE HE STUDIES FOR HOURS AT A TIME. A PLAN IS FORMING.

A FAIR WIND BRINGS THEM TO THE ISLAND OF MENORCA AND THERE, IN A SHELTERED BAY, LIES ALETA'S FLEET OF SHIPS, STORM-DRIVEN OFF THEIR COURSE AND AWAITING A FAVORABLE BREEZE.

THIS IS GREAT GOOD FORTUNE, FOR NOT ONLY ARE THEY TOGETHER AGAIN WEEKS SOONER, BUT FROM HERE VAL CAN PUT HIS PLANS INTO ACTION, AND THEY ARE BOLD PLANS.

HE PINS ONE OF HIS MAPS ON THE WALL AND WITH RED CHALK DRAWS A LINE. "THIS IS THE PRESENT ROUTE FROM HERE TO BRITAIN," HE SAYS. THEN WITH BLUE CHALK TRACES ANOTHER LINE. "THIS IS THE NEW WAY I PROPOSE TO EXPLORE. IF AN OVERLAND ROAD CAN BE BUILT, IT WILL SAVE MORE THAN A THOUSAND MILES OF SEA VOYAGE!"

HAL FOSTER

ONCE MORE VAL AND PRINCE ARN SET OFF AT ADVENTURE. ALETA SIGHS. OH, WELL, SHE WON'T BE LONELY, FOR HER HUSBAND HAS LEFT HER WITH THREE CHILDREN TO LOOK AFTER.
NEXT WEEK—**Hispania**

1-28-62

Prince Valiant
IN THE DAYS OF KING ARTHUR
WRITTEN AND ILLUSTRATED BY HAROLD R FOSTER

Our Story: WHERE THE PYRENEES MOUNTAINS COME DOWN TO THE SEA THERE IS A TOWN, AND HERE PRINCE VALIANT GOES ASHORE. TO THE SOUTH LIES HISPANIA (SPAIN), ON THE NORTH GAUL (FRANCE). HE SECURES HORSES AND A GUIDE.

THE TRAIL IS STEEP AND ROUGH, UNFIT FOR THE TRADE ROUTE FROM SEA TO SEA HE WISHES TO ESTABLISH.

"SUCH A ROAD IS POSSIBLE TO THE SOUTH, BUT THE VISIGOTHS OVERRUN THE LAND AND AN ARMY COULD NOT KEEP THE WAY SAFE," THEIR GUIDE TELLS THEM.

"THERE IS A ROAD IN THE SOUTH OF GAUL THAT FOLLOWS THE GARONNE RIVER. WAR IS INCESSANT THERE AND POWERFUL CHIEFTAINS ARE BUILDING STRONG WALLS OF STONE AND TALL CASTLES TO DEFEND WHAT THEY CLAIM IS THEIRS."

VAL AND ARN STUDY THEIR CRUDE MAPS AND DECIDE TO LEAVE THE MOUNTAINS AND TRAVERSE THE LESS RUGGED FOOTHILLS.

JUSTIN HAD TAKEN HIS FATHER'S SWORD AND SHIRT OF MAIL AND GONE OFF TO WAR. NOW, TWO YEARS LATER, HE RETURNS HOMEWARD, RICHER ONLY BY HIS SCARS.

NUMBLY HE SITS AMID THE WRECKAGE OF HIS FATHER'S HOUSE. HE KNOWS ONLY TOO WELL, FROM GRIM EXPERIENCE, WHAT HAPPENS TO A VILLAGE WHEN WAR COMES.

HE IS AROUSED FROM DESPAIR BY THE SMELL OF FOOD. HIS NOSE, SHARPENED BY MONTHS OF HUNGER, LEADS HIM TO THE SOURCE. QUIETLY HE DRAWS HIS SWORD.

NEXT WEEK - **The Demon**

1304.

2-4-62

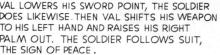

Our Story: PRINCE VALIANT PULLS UP HIS COIF AND DRAWS THE 'SINGING SWORD' AS THE ARMED WARRIOR APPROACHES. LINES OF SORROW AND DESPAIR ARE ETCHED ON HIS FACE AND HIS HUNGRY EYES STARE AT THE FOOD.

VAL LOWERS HIS SWORD POINT, THE SOLDIER DOES LIKEWISE. THEN VAL SHIFTS HIS WEAPON TO HIS LEFT HAND AND RAISES HIS RIGHT PALM OUT. THE SOLDIER FOLLOWS SUIT, THE SIGN OF PEACE.

VAL SHEATHES HIS SWORD AND WITH A WAVE OF HIS HAND INVITES THE MAN TO SHARE HIS REPAST. THERE CAN BE NO DOUBT THAT HE IS ON THE VERGE OF STARVATION.

ONLY WHEN HIS HUNGER IS SATISFIED DOES HE TALK. THEN, POINTING TO THE LUSH LANDS BELOW THEM, HE TELLS OF INCESSANT WARS, BRUTAL AND RUINOUS; OF CHIEFTAINS LEAVING THEIR STRONG-HOLDS TO LAY WASTE THE HOLDINGS OF THEIR NEIGHBORS.

THEIR GUIDE REFUSES TO GO FARTHER. HE PREFERS THE DOUBTFUL SAFETY OF THE RUG-GED MOUNTAINS TO THE CERTAINTY OF BEING MURDERED IN THE LOWLANDS.

SO THE GUIDE IS PAID OFF AND JUSTIN VOL-UNTEERS TO TAKE HIS PLACE. AFTER THE DULL MISERY OF WARFARE THIS IS LIKE A HOLIDAY.

1305

THEN TERROR STRIKES! GUARDING A WELL-WORN PATH IS THE HUGE AND MENACING FIGURE OF A GIANT, OR IS IT A TROLL? NEXT WEEK— **The Mysterious Ruin**

2-11-62

Prince Valiant
IN THE DAYS OF KING ARTHUR

WRITTEN AND ILLUSTRATED BY HAROLD R FOSTER

Our Story: TERROR HOLDS THEM IN ITS GRIP. THEN, WITH TREMBLING HAND PRINCE VALIANT GUIDES HIS HORSE TOWARD THE TOWERING HORROR. FOR HE HAS REMEMBERED WISE MERLIN'S TEACHING; THAT THE SEEMINGLY WEIRD OR UNUSUAL GENERALLY HAS A LOGICAL EXPLANATION.

AS HE CAUTIOUSLY ADVANCES, VAL GAINS CONFIDENCE, FOR HIS HORSE SHOWS NO SIGN OF NERVOUSNESS, AS IT WOULD WERE THE FIGURE A LIVING THING.

PLASTER! BUT TURNED OUT BY THE HAND OF A MASTER CRAFTSMAN. VAL IS CURIOUS. WHAT LIES AHEAD ON THIS PATH THAT SUCH A GUARDIAN BE SET HERE TO SCARE AWAY INTRUDERS?

HE RIDES UP THE TRAIL AND COMES TO A WIDE VALLEY WHERE CULTIVATED FIELDS AND GARDENS RIPEN IN THE SUN AND FLOCKS OF SHEEP GRAZE ON THE HILLSIDE. THERE IS NO SIGN OF HOUSES OR WORKERS.

WHEN VAL RETURNS TO ARN AND JUSTIN HE IS THOUGHTFUL. *"THAT FIGURE IS TO FRIGHTEN INTRUDERS FROM THE PATH THAT LEADS UP TO FIELDS AND PASTURE, SO WE WILL FOLLOW IT DOWNWARD AND SEE WHAT IS AT THE OTHER END."*

HIGH ON A ROCKY SPUR STANDS A GUTTED AND FIRE-BLACKENED MONASTERY, GRIM EVIDENCE THAT THE VISIGOTHS HAVE PASSED THIS WAY.

BUT THE PATH ENDS ON A PLATEAU, WHILE THE STEPS LEADING TO THE CRUMBLING RUIN ARE WEED-GROWN FROM DISUSE.

NEXT WEEK- **The Fearful Cavern**

1306

HAL FOSTER

2-18-62

Prince Valiant

IN THE DAYS OF KING ARTHUR

WRITTEN AND ILLUSTRATED BY Harold R Foster

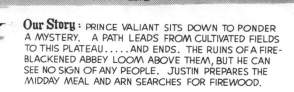

Our Story: PRINCE VALIANT SITS DOWN TO PONDER A MYSTERY. A PATH LEADS FROM CULTIVATED FIELDS TO THIS PLATEAU.....AND ENDS. THE RUINS OF A FIRE-BLACKENED ABBEY LOOM ABOVE THEM, BUT HE CAN SEE NO SIGN OF ANY PEOPLE. JUSTIN PREPARES THE MIDDAY MEAL AND ARN SEARCHES FOR FIREWOOD.

A PILE OF BRUSHWOOD PROMISES A PLENTIFUL SUPPLY, BUT WHEN HE ATTEMPTS TO PULL SOME LOOSE, THE WHOLE MASS TOPPLES FORWARD REVEALING THE MOUTH OF A CAVE.

ARN SCREAMS WITH TERROR AS NIGHTMARE MONSTERS GLOWER AT HIM FROM THE DARKNESS.

EVEN VAL'S COURAGE MIGHT HAVE FAILED HIM HAD THEY NOT BEEN FRIGHTENED ONCE BEFORE THAT DAY BY A FIGURE OF PLASTER. THESE TOO ARE THE WORK OF MEN AND NOT FROM THE UNDER-WORLD.

"A MASTER SCULPTOR, MANY ASSISTANTS. FEAR IS THEIR DEFENSE, THEREFORE WEAK AT ARMS: THE TUNNEL LEADS UPWARD TOWARD THE ABBEY, SO WE WILL VISIT IT. BUT WE WILL NOT RISK THIS DARK WAY."

JUSTIN FOLLOWS CLOSE BEHIND VAL, SHAKING WITH FEAR, FOR TO HIS SUPERSTITIOUS MIND, EVEN THE PLASTER DEMONS HAVE THE POWER OF EVIL.

1307

HAL FOSTER

"PUT UP YOUR SWORDS," SAYS VAL. "I DO NOT DOUBT THAT WE ARE BEING WATCHED, SO SHOW THAT WE COME IN PEACE."

NEXT WEEK— **The Abbot**

2-25-62

Prince Valiant
IN THE DAYS OF KING ARTHUR

WRITTEN AND ILLUSTRATED BY HAROLD R FOSTER

Our Story: PRINCE VALIANT, ARN AND JUSTIN CLIMB THE BROKEN, WEED-GROWN STAIRWAY TO THE GUTTED MONASTERY. THEY EXPECTED MORE HORRORS LIKE THOSE GRAVEN IMAGES THAT HAD SO FRIGHTENED THEM IN THE CAVERN.

THE NAVE OF THE ABBEY IS CHOKED WITH DEBRIS, BUT AT THE FAR END THE CHOIR AND ALTAR ARE INTACT, SWEPT CLEAN AND SHOWING SIGNS OF BEING WELL USED.

AS BECOMES A CHRISTIAN KNIGHT AND A FELLOW OF THE ROUND TABLE, VAL KNEELS BEFORE THE ALTAR TO REDEDICATE HIS SWORD TO THE SERVICE OF HIS KING AND HIS GOD.

A DOOR IN THE CHANCEL OPENS AND AN ABBOT APPEARS. *"WE BID A MOST HEARTY WELCOME TO CHRISTIAN GENTLEMEN. IT IS SELDOM IN THESE WARLIKE DAYS THAT WE HAVE VISITORS WHO COME IN PEACE."*

"WE HAVE LEFT THE ABBEY IN RUINS, SO PASSING WAR BANDS WILL THINK THE WHOLE MONASTERY ABANDONED AND LEAVE US IN PEACE," EXPLAINS THE ABBOT. *"WE KEEP HIDDEN BEHIND OUR WALLS. ONLY THOSE WHO TILL OUR FIELDS LEAVE BY THE SECRET PASSAGE BEFORE DAWN AND RETURN AFTER DARK."*

1308

BUT EVEN AS HE SPEAKS A WAR BAND IS LOOKING THEIR WAY. FOR A SCOUT HAD SEEN VAL AND HIS COMPANIONS ENTER THE ABBEY.
NEXT WEEK— **The Warning Cry**

HAL FOSTER

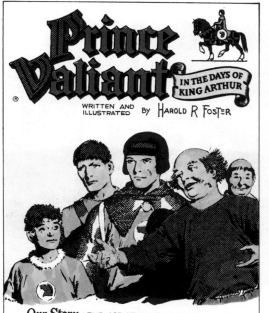

Prince Valiant
IN THE DAYS OF KING ARTHUR
WRITTEN AND ILLUSTRATED By HAROLD R FOSTER

Our Story: THE ABBOT HAD LIVED THROUGH THAT AWFUL DAY WHEN THE MONASTERY WAS SACKED AND BURNED, AND HE IS JUSTLY PROUD OF THE RESTORATION HE AND THE OTHER SURVIVORS HAVE ACCOMPLISHED.

"OUR ORDER SENDS SCHOLARS AND TEACHERS OUT INTO THE WORLD TO KEEP THE LAMPS OF LEARNING BRIGHT IN THIS DARK AGE. AMONG THESE BROTHERS ARE OUR MASONS, WEAVERS, COOKS, FARMERS AND OTHER CRAFTSMEN."

"AND THIS IS BROTHER JOHN, OUR SCULPTOR. HIS IMAGES OF SAINTS AND MARTYRS ADORN THE HIGH ALTAR AND HIS PLASTER DEMONS FRIGHTEN AWAY INTRUDERS."
"I KNOW," ANSWERS VAL, "FOR THEY ALMOST FRIGHTENED US WITLESS."

THE ABBOT IS AS HAPPY AS A SCHOOLBOY ON A HOLIDAY, FOR IT IS ALL TOO SELDOM THAT HE HAS A VISITOR TO WHOM HE CAN DISPLAY WHAT THE BROTHERS HAVE ACCOMPLISHED. THEN COMES THE CRY OF WARNING.

A SLENDER YOUTH IN RICH ATTIRE IS GALLOPING UP THE ROCKY PATH CRYING CHEERFULLY: "THE GOTHS ARE COMING!"

1309

THE WAR BAND EMERGES FROM THE DARK FOREST AND CLIMBS STEADILY UPWARD, THE SUN GLEAMING OFF A THOUSAND SPEAR POINTS.

"NOW, BROTHER JOHN, YOU HAVE A CHANCE TO UNVEIL YOUR MASTERPIECE. WE WILL ALL PRAY FOR YOUR SUCCESS, FOR THE LIVES OF OUR BROTHERS ARE AT STAKE."

NEXT WEEK- **The Moment of Peril**

3-11-62

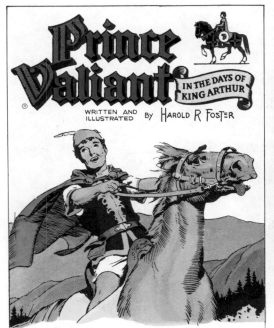

Prince Valiant
IN THE DAYS OF KING ARTHUR
WRITTEN AND ILLUSTRATED BY HAROLD R FOSTER

Our Story: "THE GOTHS ARE COMING, PREPARE A WELCOME!" SHOUTS A YOUTH AS HE URGES HIS TIRED MOUNT UP THE STEEP PATH TO THE MONASTERY.

"PRINCE VALIANT, MEET STEPHAN, A WORLDLY YOUTH WHO SHOWS LITTLE SIGN OF REPENTANCE," SIGHS THE ABBOT, "BUT THANKS FOR THE TIMELY WARNING."

THE GOTHS FOLLOW, A THOUSAND STRONG. THEY HAVE SEEN MEN AMID THE RUINS OF THE ABBEY, AND WHERE THERE ARE MEN THERE IS LOOT OR, BETTER STILL, FOOD.

UNTIL THEY LEFT THEIR NORTHERN FORESTS THIS WARBAND HAD NEVER SEEN A BUILDING LARGER THAN A COTTAGE. NOW, AFTER TWO YEARS OF WANDERING ACROSS PLUNDERED GAUL, TALL BUILDINGS OF STONE MEAN FORTS OR CASTLES, HARD FIGHTING AND DEFEAT.

IN A CRYPT BELOW THE CHAPEL JUSTIN, WITH FLINT AND STRIKING IRON, SENDS A SPARK INTO A HEAP OF STRAW WHICH BROTHER JOHN BLOWS INTO A FLAME, AND THE SMOKE ASCENDS TO OPENINGS IN THE CEILING.

FROM A WINDOW IN A GALLERY ABOVE THE ABBEY VAL AND ARN LOOK DOWN. THE SQUARE STRUCTURE BEFORE THE CHAPEL, WHICH VAL THOUGHT WAS A CONFESSIONAL, BEGINS TO SMOKE.

THE PAGAN WARBAND CROWD THE ENTRANCE AND CLIMB THE HEAP OF DEBRIS. AWED BY THE SILENT EMPTINESS, THEY ADVANCE SLOWLY TO WHERE GOLD AND SILVER SHINE ON THE ALTAR. THEN A PUFF OF SMOKE HALTS THEM.

NEXT WEEK— **The Monster**

3-18-62

Prince Valiant
IN THE DAYS OF KING ARTHUR
WRITTEN AND ILLUSTRATED BY Harold R Foster

Our Story : FROM A WINDOW HIGH IN THE GALLERY PRINCE VALIANT AND ARN LOOK DOWN AT THE PAGAN WARBAND AS THEY SURGE FORWARD. THEY ARE STRANGELY QUIET AS IF OVERAWED BY THE STILL, SILENT GRANDEUR OF THE RUINED ABBEY.

THEN A CLOUD OF SMOKE BELLOWS UP FROM THE WOODEN SCREEN, WHICH OPENS, SEALING OFF THE ALTAR. FOR A MOMENT THE WHOLE END OF THE BUILDING IS OBSCURED, AND THIS IS ENOUGH IN ITSELF TO BRING FEAR TO THE PRIMITIVE MINDS OF THE BARBARIANS.

HAL FOSTER

A GASP OF HORROR RUNS THROUGH THE PAGAN THRONG AS A SHADOWY FORM APPEARS DIMLY IN THE SWIRLING CLOUD. THEN THE SMOKE THINS, REVEALING A MONSTER SO HUGE AND MENACING THAT PANIC AKIN TO MADNESS GRIPS THE WATCHERS AND, SCREAMING, THEY TRAMPLE EACH OTHER IN A WILD SCRAMBLE TO ESCAPE.

NEXT WEEK- **The Dancers**

3-25-6

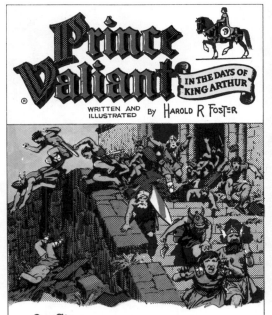

Prince Valiant
IN THE DAYS OF KING ARTHUR
WRITTEN AND ILLUSTRATED BY HAROLD R FOSTER

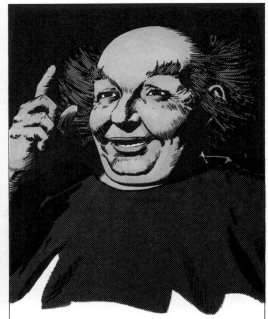

Our Story: FROM OUT OF A CLOUD OF SMOKE (THAT SMELLS SUSPICIOUSLY LIKE WET STRAW BURNING) THERE APPEARS A TERRIBLE DRAGON, AND THE SAVAGE WAR-BAND FLEE IN SCREAMING TERROR.

THE GENTLE BROTHERS WATCH IN GLEE AS THE GOTHS GO LEAPING DOWN THE MOUNTAINSIDE, CARELESS OF BROKEN BONES AND LOST WEAPONS.

"NOW WE WILL REPAIR TO THE CHAPEL AND GIVE THANKS FOR OUR DELIVERANCE," ANNOUNCES THE ABBOT, "AND WE MUST COMMEND BROTHER JOHN ON HIS ARTISTRY."

BUT BROTHER JOHN IS ALREADY GIVING THANKS IN HIS OWN WAY. SINGING A CATCHY DITTY HE IS DANCING A JIG AROUND HIS PLASTER DRAGON.

"BROTHER JOHN, CEASE!", THUNDERS THE ABBOT. "YOUR UNSEEMLY LEVITY DOES NOT BECOME ONE OF OUR ORDER. WORLDLY PRIDE IS A SIN, SEEK GRACE IN THE PRACTICE OF HUMILITY!"

"OH, THESE ARTISTS!" COMPLAINS THE ABBOT, "THEY ARE ALL ALIKE; FRIVOLOUS, FULL OF VAINGLORY AND CONCEIT. THERE IS NO TRUE PENITENCE IN THEM!"

ALL THROUGH THE EVENING MEAL THE ABBOT SEEMS LOST IN THOUGHT. "NOW, HOW DID IT GO?" HE IS HEARD TO MUTTER AS HE WAVES HIS WOODEN SPOON.

BUT THAT NIGHT WHEN PRINCE VALIANT AND HIS SON PASS THE ENTRANCE TO HIS CELL, THEY HEAR HIM EXCLAIM: "AH, NOW I REMEMBER IT!" THEN THEY TIPTOE AWAY AND LEAVE THE ABBOT TO HIS LITTLE MOMENT OF WORLDLY JOY.
NEXT WEEK- The Gay Fugitive

1312.

4-1-62

Prince Valiant

IN THE DAYS OF KING ARTHUR

WRITTEN AND ILLUSTRATED BY HAROLD R FOSTER

Our Story: AT LAST COMES THE HOUR OF PARTING. PRINCE VALIANT AND ARN BID FARE-WELL TO THE PEACEFUL BROTHERS AND LEAVE THE MONASTERY BY WAY OF THE SECRET TUNNEL. JUSTIN SHUDDERS AS HE PASSES THE AWFUL IMAGES THAT GUARD THE PASSAGEWAY.

JUSTIN LOOKS BACK. WAR, BRUTALITY, HUNGER AND PAIN ARE THE LOT OF THE MERCENARY SOLDIER. HOW HE LONGS FOR THE PEACE AND SERENITY HE IS LEAVING BEHIND.

STEPHAN LEADS THE WAY OVER THE FAINT GOAT TRAILS HE HAS KNOWN SINCE CHILDHOOD. "LOOK," HE EXCLAIMS, "THERE GOES THE GOTH WARBAND. THEY HAVE FOUND THE PASS AND ARE GOING OVER THE MOUNTAINS INTO HISPANIA, AND WE WILL BE WELL RID OF THEM."

THROUGH THE PASS ABOVE THE VILLAGE OF RONCESVALLES THE WAR-BAND WINDS LIKE A GLITTERING SERPENT. HERE, THREE CENTURIES LATER, THE MIGHTY CHARLEMAGNE WILL MEET WITH DEFEAT, AND ROLAND DIE A HERO'S DEATH.

ONE DAY THEY LOOK DOWN ON A WALLED CITY, ITS TOWERS AND BASTIONS AGLOW IN THE SUNSET. "THERE RULES SADONICK, DUKE OF AQUELOEN, ON THE DUCAL THRONE RIGHTLY MINE," SAYS STEPHAN.

1313.

"THE FALSE DUKE HAS MURDERED EVERY RELATIVE THAT MIGHT THREATEN HIS RULE. I, THE RIGHTFUL DUKE, HAVE BEEN A FUGITIVE FROM HIS ASSASSINS SINCE CHILDHOOD."

IN THE MORNING THEY PART, STEPHAN TO GO BY SECRET WAYS TO ONCE AGAIN SEE HIS MOTHER, AND VAL, DESPITE ALL WARN-INGS, TO ENTER THE WALLED CITY.

NEXT WEEK— **The Duke**

4-8-62

Prince Valiant
IN THE DAYS OF KING ARTHUR
WRITTEN AND ILLUSTRATED BY HAROLD R FOSTER

Our Story: DESPITE STEPHAN'S WARNING, PRINCE VALIANT RIDES THROUGH THE CITY GATES OF DUKE SADONICK'S STRONGHOLD. FOR VAL CANNOT BELIEVE THAT THE DUKE COULD BE SO EVIL A RULER AS STEPHAN HAS DESCRIBED.

WHEN ONE NOBLE CROSSES THE DOMAIN OF ANOTHER, IT IS CUSTOMARY TO PAY THE RULING ONE A COURTESY CALL.

THE DUKE IS AT WORK, AND ARN'S EYES GROW BIG WITH HORROR. EXCEPT FOR A HARDENING OF HIS JAW, VAL'S EXPRESSION DOES NOT CHANGE.......

FOR THE DUKE IS SITTING AMONG A NEAT ARRAY OF GLEAMING INSTRUMENTS, AND BEFORE HIM, STRETCHED UPON THE RACK, IS THE LIMP FORM OF ONE OF HIS UNFORTUNATE ENEMIES.

DUKE SADONICK WIPES HIS HANDS ON A WHITE NAPKIN AND GREETS HIS GUESTS. *"I CAN SEE YOU HAVE THE ARTISTIC TOUCH,"* COMPLIMENTS VAL. *"AH, YES,"* ANSWERS THE DUKE MODESTLY, *"I DO HAVE SOME TALENT, AND DISPLAYING IT THUS INSURES THE LOYALTY OF MY COURTIERS."*

REFRESHMENTS ARE ORDERED AND VAL MUST ANSWER MANY SHREWD QUESTIONS.

THEY ARE SHOWN TO THEIR QUARTERS AND JUSTIN BRINGS IN THEIR SADDLEBAGS.
"GUARD YOUR TONGUES," VAL ORDERS. *"THE DUKE HAS AN ARMY OF SPIES, OUR EVERY WORD IS REPORTED. HE EVEN KNOWS STEPHAN IS NEAR, AND WE KNOW THE DOOM IN STORE FOR HIM WERE HE TAKEN!"*

NEXT WEEK— **Bait for the Trap**

1314.

4-15-62

Prince Valiant
IN THE DAYS OF KING ARTHUR
®
WRITTEN AND
ILLUSTRATED BY HAROLD R FOSTER

Our Story: PRINCE VALIANT FINDS HIM-
SELF THE GUEST OF DUKE SADONICK, AND
HIS HOST HAS GREAT CHARM AND IS BRIL-
LIANT IN CONVERSATION. IT IS HARD TO
BELIEVE HIM THE SAME MAN WHO, ONLY
YESTERDAY, TORTURED A VICTIM ON THE
RACK . . . . .

. . . . . . UNTIL VAL DISAGREES WITH HIM
ON SOME MINOR POINT. THEN HIS FACE
HARDENS, HIS EYES GLITTER WITH RAGE,
AND VAL IS GLAD WHEN THE MEETING IS
OVER.

ONE THING IS CERTAIN. THE DUKE IS
MAD WITH POWER AND WILL BROOK NO
OPPOSITION TO HIS WILL, AND THERE IS
ONLY ONE WHO STANDS IN HIS WAY . . .
STEPHAN!

FEAR HAS TURNED EVERY COURTIER INTO AN INFORMER, EVERY
SERVANT A SPY. ONLY IN THE SPACIOUS COURTYARD CAN THEY SPEAK
TOGETHER WITHOUT BEING OVERHEARD. *"WE MAY HAVE TO LEAVE
THIS MISCHANCY PLACE SUDDENLY,"* SAYS VAL, *"AND WE WILL
NEED OUR MOUNTS OUTSIDE THE GATES."*

VAL'S VOICE IS RAISED IN ANGER SO ALL CAN HEAR; *"I TOLD
YOU TO KEEP THE HORSES IN GOOD CONDITION, KNAVE. EXERCISE
THEM! TWICE DAILY RUN THEM IN THE MEADOW BELOW THE CITY
GATES."* JUSTIN MOUNTS SULLENLY AND RIDES OUT.

THE GATEKEEPERS BECOME USED TO THE
COMING AND GOING OF JUSTIN AND PAY
LITTLE ATTENTION TO HIM.

NOW THAT THEY HAVE STAYED THE NUMBER
OF DAYS DEMANDED BY COURTESY, VAL AND
ARN BID THE DUKE FAREWELL.

1315.

HAL FOSTER

*"BUT NO, SIR VALIANT, I HAVE NEED OF
YOU AND THE YOUNG PRINCE TO BAIT A
TRAP FOR STEPHAN. YOU RECOGNIZE
THE NECESSITY, I HOPE, FOR STEPHAN
STANDS IN MY WAY."*
NEXT WEEK- **The Hostage**

4-22-62

Prince Valiant
IN THE DAYS OF KING ARTHUR
WRITTEN AND ILLUSTRATED BY HAROLD R FOSTER

Our Story: THE DUKE IS SMILING AS HE INFORMS PRINCE VALIANT: *"ONLY STEPHAN STANDS IN MY WAY. HE IS NOW VISITING HIS MOTHER'S FORTRESS CASTLE. YOU ARE TO GO TO HIM AND, AS A TRUSTED FRIEND, DECOY HIM OUT INTO OUR AMBUSH."*

"AND TO INSURE THAT YOU WILL OBEY OUR WILL FAITHFULLY, YOUR SON ARN WILL BE CHAINED BESIDE THE RACK UNTIL YOU RETURN."

VAL STRIVES TO FORM PLANS OF ESCAPE, ONLY TO ABANDON EACH IN TURN. FINALLY IN DESPERATION HE WHISPERS TO JUSTIN: *"FIND THE WAY TO STEPHAN AND WHEN NEXT YOU EXERCISE THE HORSES BEYOND THE GATES, RIDE TO HIM WITH A WARNING!"*

SO JUSTIN DECAMPS WITH THE THREE HORSES. AND HE SPEEDS BACK ALONG THE WAY THEY HAD COME UNTIL HE REACHES THE SPOT WHERE THEY PARTED FROM STEPHAN. THEN HE FOLLOWS THE GOAT TRACK STEPHAN HAD TAKEN ALONG THE MOUNTAIN SIDE.

IT IS A FULL DAY BEFORE VAL DISCOVERS THAT HIS FALSE SQUIRE HAS STOLEN ALL THEIR HORSES, AND HIS ANGER SEEMS ALMOST REAL AS HE OFFERS A RICH REWARD FOR HIS CAPTURE.

BUT THE DUKE IS SUSPICIOUS: *"COULD YOU HAVE SENT HIM TO WARN STEPHAN?"* HE ASKS. *"WELL, HARDLY!"* GRUMBLES VAL, *"FOR THE KNAVE TOOK ALL OUR MOUNTS, OUR ONLY MEANS OF ESCAPE."*

VAL IS SAVED FROM FURTHER QUESTIONING BY THE ARRIVAL OF THE CHAMBERLAIN, AND THE WHISPERED MESSAGE HE BRINGS CAUSES THE DUKE TO SMILE EVILLY.

NEXT WEEK- **A Time of Terror**

1316.

4-29-62

Prince Valiant

IN THE DAYS OF KING ARTHUR

WRITTEN AND ILLUSTRATED BY HAROLD R FOSTER

Our Story : IN THE TOWN OF AQUELOEN DUKE SADONICK RULES BY SHEER TERROR, AND DEATH COMES MOST HORRIBLY TO THOSE WHO CROSS HIS WILL. ONLY HIS NEPHEW, STEPHAN, STANDS BETWEEN HIM AND ABSOLUTE RULE.

AND THE DUKE HAS CHOSEN PRINCE VALIANT TO BETRAY STEPHAN TO HIS DEATH. ARN IS TO BE HELD AS A HOSTAGE TO ASSURE THE AWFUL DEED IS DONE.

IT FALLS TO JUSTIN'S LOT TO CARRY VAL'S WARNING TO STEPHAN. WELL HE KNOWS THAT THE DUKE HAS SPIES EVERYWHERE, SO HE LEAVES THE HORSES WITH A SHEPHERD AND BORROWS HIS SMOCK.

IT WOULD BE IMPOSSIBLE FOR A HUMBLE SHEPHERD TO GAIN AUDIENCE WITH A NOBLEMAN, BUT JUSTIN IS IN LUCK. HE MEETS STEPHAN AS HE RIDES A-HAWKING.

"THE DUKE PROMISED DEATH ON THE RACK FOR YOUNG ARN UNLESS PRINCE VALIANT AGREED TO BETRAY YOU INTO HIS EVIL HANDS." STEPHAN IS THOUGHTFUL. "THIS IS TERRIBLE," HE SAYS, "FOR THE DUKE IS LIKE A MAD DOG AND WILL KILL ALL WHO FAIL HIS COMMANDS."

"HE WILL NOT TRY TO STORM THE CASTLE. HE HAS TRIED AND FAILED; IT IS ONLY BY TREACHERY..... TREACHERY! WHY CANNOT WE TRY TREACHERY, TOO?"

1317.

"MOTHER, GET READY TO GO WITH ME TO OUR HUNTING LODGE. WE WILL TAKE A FEW FRIENDS AND SERVANTS AND STAY FOR A WEEK.".

AND THIS IS THE NEWS A SPY BRINGS TO THE DUKE AND CAUSES HIM TO SMILE HIS EVIL, TRIUMPHANT SMILE.

NEXT WEEK- **A-Hunting we will go!**

5-6-62

Prince Valiant
IN THE DAYS OF KING ARTHUR
WRITTEN AND ILLUSTRATED BY HAROLD R FOSTER

Our Story: SOLDIERS GATHER BELOW THE CITY'S WALLS. TO PRINCE VALIANT'S PRACTICED EYE THE TROOP IS NOT LARGE ENOUGH FOR AN ASSAULT, SO THE DUKE MUST BE PLANNING FOR A RAID OR AMBUSH.

HE IS NOT LONG IN FINDING OUT. "WE RIDE AT DAWN," SAYS THE DUKE WITH A CRUEL SMILE, "AND YOU MAY FULFILL YOUR TASK WITHOUT STAIN TO YOUR HONOR. MEANWHILE, YOUR SON WILL BE CHAINED BESIDE THE RACK TO INSURE YOUR OBEDIENCE."

AT DAWN DUKE SADONICK LEADS FORTH HIS PICKED TROOP, AND VAL, IN HOPELESS RAGE, RIDES WITH HIM. A QUICK SWORD STROKE WOULD FINISH THE DUKE, BUT IT WOULD ALSO BRING ABOUT HIS SON'S DEATH BY TORTURE.

AND AT THE SAME HOUR STEPHAN AND HIS MOTHER ARE RIDING TO THEIR HUNTING LODGE. "YOU ARE JUST LIKE YOUR LATE FATHER," SHE SCOLDS, "ALWAYS THINKING OF SPORT. WHY DID YOU NOT STAY IN THE MONASTERY WHERE YOU WERE SAFE FROM YOUR UNCLE?"

"UNCLE SADONICK IS A VERY TREACHEROUS MAN, BUT," HE ADDS PIOUSLY, "I DO HOPE NOTHING BAD HAPPENS TO HIM." THEN HE CHUCKLES.

THE HUNTING PARTY IS SETTLED COMFORTABLY FOR THE NIGHT AND, HAD IT NOT BEEN FOR HIS MOTHER'S STEADY PRATTLE, HE MIGHT HAVE HEARD.....

.....THE BUSHES RUSTLING AS A HUNDRED ARMED MEN SURROUND THE QUIET HUNTING LODGE.

NEXT WEEK- **The Reluctant Sword**   5-13-62

Prince Valiant
IN THE DAYS OF KING ARTHUR
WRITTEN AND ILLUSTRATED BY HAROLD R FOSTER

Our Story: STEPHAN AND HIS MOTHER LOOK UP AS THE DOOR OPENS AND THERE IN THE FLICKERING CANDLELIGHT STANDS DUKE SADONICK, HIS CRUEL FACE ALIGHT WITH TRIUMPH.

FOLLOWED BY A DOZEN ARMED BULLIES, HE SEATS HIMSELF. *"YOU HAVE AVOIDED ME ALL THESE YEARS, STEPHAN; NOW MY TURN HAS COME. SIR VALIANT! RID ME OF MY TROUBLESOME NEPHEW!"*

AS VAL HESITATES, THE DUKE'S FACE BECOMES DARK WITH ANGER. *"YOUR OWN SON AND HEIR STANDS CHAINED TO THE RACK. REFUSE MY BIDDING AND YOU SIGN HIS DEATH WARRANT."*

TO SAVE ARN FROM A HORRIBLE DEATH HE MUST DO A DEED THAT WILL BLIGHT HIS HONOR AND SCAR HIS VERY SOUL. HE DRAWS THE 'SINGING SWORD' AND IT COMES MOANING FROM ITS SCABBARD AND HANGS LEADEN IN HIS HAND, A LIFELESS THING.

THEN VAL STEPS IN FRONT OF STEPHAN AND FACES THE DUKE HIS FACE RESOLUTE, THE LUST FOR BATTLE IN HIS EYES, HE STRIKES THE TABLE WITH THE GLITTERING BLADE AND ONCE MORE IT SINGS, EAGER, TRIUMPHANT!

"GUARDS! KILL THEM, KILL THEM ALL!" SCREAMS THE DUKE. AS THE GUARDS HESITATE BEFORE THE BRIGHT MENACE OF THE SWORD, A TRUMPET SOUNDS.

THE SILENCE OF THE NIGHT IS SHATTERED BY ANGRY SHOUTS AND THE CLASH OF ARMS. STEPHAN POINTS TO THE DOOR. *"MY MEN WERE IN THE FOREST AWAITING YOUR EXPECTED ARRIVAL, DEAR UNCLE, SO THE TRICKSTER HAS BEEN TRICKED!"*

NEXT WEEK- **A Ride for Life**

1319.

5-20-62

Prince Valiant
IN THE DAYS OF KING ARTHUR

WRITTEN AND ILLUSTRATED BY HAROLD R FOSTER

Our Story: SADONICK, FALSE DUKE OF AQUELOEN, SITS QUIETLY WHILE STEPHAN'S MEN DISARM HIS BODYGUARD AND LEAD THEM AWAY. AND ALL THIS TIME STEPHAN'S MOTHER HAS GONE CALMLY ON WITH HER EMBROIDERY, BUT NOW HER PATIENCE IS AT AN END.

"SADONICK, YOU ARE AN INFERNAL NUISANCE, WHAT WITH ALL YOUR NOISE AND BLUSTERING YOU HAVE MADE ME BOTCH MY SEWING. STEPHAN, TAKE HIM OUT AND CUT OFF HIS HEAD, PLEASE."

SO MERCIFUL AN END WOULD NOT BE HIS. THE AWFUL CRUELTIES HE HAD INFLICTED WOULD CRY FOR VENGEANCE, A MORE LINGERING VENGEANCE.

PRINCE VALIANT SEES THE FURTIVE LOOK AS HE STEALTHILY TAKES A VIAL FROM HIS POUCH AND REMOVES THE STOPPER. THEN THE 'SINGING SWORD' FLASHES OUT.

"AN EASY DEATH BY POISON IS NOT FOR YOU. YOU ORDERED MY SON CHAINED TO THE RACK AS HOSTAGE FOR MY OBEDIENCE. SHOULD ANY HARM COME TO HIM, YOU WILL DIE ON YOUR OWN RACK!"

THEN HE MOUNTS AND RACES THROUGH THE NIGHT IN FRANTIC HASTE TO REACH AQUELOEN BEFORE NEWS OF THE DUKE'S CAPTURE ARRIVES.

AT DAWN A SPENT HORSE AND WEARY RIDER PASS THROUGH THE CITY GATES. ARE THEY TOO LATE?

1320.

VAL TOSSES THE REINS TO THE DIRTY-FACED STABLE BOY AND STRIDES INTO THE CASTLE TO FIND AN ANSWER TO HIS FEARS.
NEXT WEEK- **'Dirty Face'**

5-27-62

Prince Valiant
IN THE DAYS OF KING ARTHUR
WRITTEN AND ILLUSTRATED BY HAROLD R FOSTER

Our Story: WITH THE DAWN COMES PRINCE VALIANT BORN ON WINGS OF ANXIETY. STRAIGHT FOR THE DUKE'S CHAMBER OF HORRORS HE RACES. WILL HE FIND HIS SON ALREADY SUFFERING UPON THE RACK?

BUT THE CHAMBER IS EMPTY SAVE FOR THE DUKE'S ASSISTANT TORMENTORS, WHO COWER IN A CORNER.

"WE COULD NOT FIND YOUR SON. WE DID NOT CARRY OUT OUR MASTER'S ORDERS. SAVE US, SIR, OR WE MUST FACE THE DUKE'S ANGER!"

HE BIDS A TRUMPETER SOUND THE CALL AND WHEN ALL HAVE GATHERED IN THE HALL: "FIND MY SON, PRINCE ARN!" HE COMMANDS. "SEARCH EVERY CORNER OF THE CASTLE AND TOWN!" THEN, WHEN THEY HESITATE, ANNOUNCES: "SADONICK NO LONGER RULES HERE, HE IS IN THE HANDS OF STEPHAN, THE REAL DUKE."

VAL REMEMBERS THE MOUNT THAT HAD CARRIED HIM SO NOBLY THROUGH THE NIGHT. THE DIRTY-FACED STABLE BOY IS CARING FOR IT TENDERLY; "NOW, WHO WOULD RIDE A HORSE INTO THIS CONDITION?" HE ASKS THE ANIMAL. "I'D LIKE TO GIVE HIM RIDING LESSONS."

THE FAMILIAR VOICE, THE IMPUDENCE! VAL FIGHTS TO CONTROL HIS EMOTIONS. AT LAST HE TURNS SLOWLY......

...". YOUR FACE IS DIRTIER THAN USUAL," HE SAYS STERNLY, "GO GET READY FOR BREAKFAST. WASH YOUR NECK AND DON'T FORGET YOUR EARS!"

ARN GOES OFF WHISTLING, AND WITH THE WEIGHT OF DESPAIR LIFTED, VAL LAUGHS AND WEEPS UNASHAMEDLY.

NEXT WEEK- **A Wall Decoration**

HAL FOSTER

1321.

6-3-62

Prince Valiant
IN THE DAYS OF KING ARTHUR
WRITTEN AND ILLUSTRATED BY HAROLD R FOSTER

Our Story: IN THE CITY OF AQUELOEN ALL THE BELLS ARE RINGING, FLAGS WAVING, AS STEPHAN, THE REAL DUKE, COMES HOME. PRINCE VALIANT IS HONORED, FOR HE HAD FACED A TERRIBLE ORDEAL--TO HOLD FAST TO HIS OATH, HIS HONOR AND HIS IDEALS AT THE RISK OF HIS SON'S LIFE.

MANY NOBLES WHO HAD SUPPORTED SADONICK WHEN HE USURPED THE DUCAL THRONE GATHER WHAT WEALTH THEY CAN ON SUCH SHORT NOTICE AND DEPART FOR LONG VACATIONS IN DISTANT LANDS.

THEN COMES THE PROBLEM OF DISPOSING OF SADONICK. BUT STEPHAN'S MATTER-OF-FACT MOTHER HAS ALREADY SOLVED THE PROBLEM. "THE DECORATION YOU SEE OVER THE MAIN GATE IS HIS HEAD, A WARNING TO EVILDOERS. THE REST OF HIM WILL BE BURIED WITH FULL HONORS AS BEFITS ONE OF NOBLE BLOOD."

A FEW MINOR OFFICIALS ARE EXECUTED IN THE MARKET PLACE TO SATISFY THE POPULAR DEMAND FOR ENTERTAINMENT; THEN STEPHAN'S RULE SETTLES DOWN INTO ROUTINE.

IT IS ABOUT THREE DAYS RIDE TO THE COAST WHERE ALETA SHOULD BE WAITING, BUT JUSTIN ASKS PERMISSION TO TURN BACK.

1322

"AS A MERCENARY I HAVE KNOWN TWO YEARS OF BRUTALITY, HUNGER AND PAIN. I LONG FOR THE PEACE AND SERENITY OF LIFE IN THE MONASTERY WHERE WE FOUND STEPHAN."

THAT IS HOW BROTHER JOHN GOT AN ASSISTANT TO HELP HIM WITH THE HORRIBLE DEMONS THAT GUARD THE MONASTERY AND ITS GENTLE BROTHERS FROM PAGAN BANDS.

NEXT WEEK-**Heads You Lose**   6-10-62

Prince Valiant
IN THE DAYS OF KING ARTHUR
WRITTEN AND ILLUSTRATED BY HAROLD R FOSTER

Our Story: THE SUNLIT STREETS OF AQUELOEN ECHO TO THE SOUNDS OF MERRIMENT, FOR THE TERRIBLE RULE OF THE FALSE DUKE SADONICK IS AT AN END AND HIS FUNERAL IS BEING CELEBRATED. HE IS BURIED IN TWO PIECES, FOR DURING HIS TRIAL HIS HEAD HAD BECOME SEPARATED FROM HIS SHOULDERS.

AT LONG LAST STEPHAN TAKES HIS RIGHTFUL PLACE ON THE DUCAL THRONE. THE CHRONICLES OF HIS TIME SHOW HIM TO BE A VERY POOR RULER, SPENDING ALL HIS TIME IN HUNTING AND FROLIC.

BUT EVEN HIS MISMANAGEMENT WAS SO MUCH BETTER THAN THE HARSH RULE OF HIS LATE UNCLE THAT HIS NAME WENT DOWN IN HISTORY AS 'STEPHAN THE GOOD.'

ONE BY ONE THE LOYAL NOBLES RETURN FROM EXILE, AND THE TRAITORS BECOME SO FEW THAT THE HEADSMAN IS ABLE TO WIPE OFF HIS AXE AND RETURN TO HIS BAKERY SHOP. THEN PRINCE VALIANT AND ARN BID FAREWELL TO STEPHAN.

VAL AND ARN CONTINUE ON THEIR WAY. SOMETIMES THEY SPEND THE NIGHT WRAPPED IN THEIR CLOAKS ON A BED OF BOUGHS; OTHER TIMES THEY ARE FORTUNATE TO HAVE A ROOF OVER THEIR HEADS.

ALL DAY VAL HAS BEEN TESTING THE WEST WIND. *"WHAT DO YOU SMELL, SIRE? I HOPE IT IS A HAUNCH OF ROAST VENISON."* *"THE SEA,"* ANSWERS HIS FATHER, *"I SMELL THE SEA!"*

THE SEA AT LAST! THEY HAVE CROSSED FROM THE MEDITERRANEAN SEA TO THE OCEAN, BUT HAVE FOUND NO SAFE ROAD FOR COMMERCE. SOMEWHERE ALONG THE SHORE ALETA IS WAITING. ARN LOOKS AT HIS ADORED HERO AND COMPANION WITH DISGUST. THERE IS A FATUOUS LOOK ON HIS FACE. *"ALETA,"* HE CAROLS, *"ALETA, ALETA!"* *"MUSH,"* MUTTERS ARN, AS HE GOES INTO A SULK.

NEXT WEEK- Mr. Whiskers

6-17-62

Prince Valiant
IN THE DAYS OF KING ARTHUR
WRITTEN AND ILLUSTRATED BY HAROLD R FOSTER

Our Story: AFTER SHE LEFT PRINCE VALIANT, ALETA HAD SAILED HER FLEET OF SHIPS AROUND SPAIN AND COME TO ANCHOR IN A SHELTERED COVE IN THE BAY OF BISCAY, THERE TO AWAIT THE ARRIVAL OF VAL AND ARN.

ALETA, AN ISLAND GIRL, HAD LEARNED TO SWIM EVEN AS SHE LEARNED TO WALK. SO IT IS NOT SURPRISING THAT HER OWN BROOD BECOME WATER-BABIES.

THEN COMES HER HOUR OF FREEDOM, TO SWIM AT RANDOM OR DIVE TO GLIDE AMONG THE WAVING SEAWEED. WATCHING HER, ONE CAN READILY BELIEVE THE LEGEND THAT SHE IS THE DESCENDANT OF A MERMAID.

AN OTTER IS THE PLAYBOY OF THE ANIMAL WORLD. HE MAKES SPORT OF EVERYTHING, AND TO FIND SOMEONE TO PLAY WITH IS JOY SUPREME.

WHERE SURF AND SAND MEET THEY COME TO REST, AND HERE HIS SENSITIVE BLACK NOSE TELLS HIM ALL ABOUT HIS NEW PLAYMATE; A FRIENDLY HUMAN, DELICIOUSLY WET AND UNAFRAID.

HE WHISTLES AND CHATTERS AN INVITATION TO COME PLAY SOME MORE AND SHE WHISTLES AND CHATTERS RIGHT BACK AT HIM. THEN HE SEES IT.....

.....ALL HIS LIFE HE HAS PLAYED WITH ROUND PEBBLES OR COLORED SHELLS, BUT THIS TOY SPARKLES AND GLEAMS AN INVITATION TO BE PUT TO SOME GOOD USE.

HIS POWERFUL JAWS SNIP THE JEWEL FROM ITS MOUNTING, AND WITH A SQUEAL OF DELIGHT, HE DIVES INTO THE WAVES, ALETA AFTER HIM. A CHASE, THIS WILL BE FUN!
NEXT WEEK - A Rival

HAL FOSTER

1324.

6-24-62

Prince Valiant
IN THE DAYS OF KING ARTHUR
WRITTEN AND ILLUSTRATED BY HAROLD R FOSTER

Our Story: PRINCE VALIANT AND ARN COME AT LAST TO THE SEA AND BEHOLD ALETA'S WAITING FLEET. AS THEY RIDE FULL GALLOP TOWARD THE LANDING PLACE VAL'S EYE CATCHES SIGHT OF A FAMILIAR SPOT OF GOLD AMID THE BLUE WAVES.

LEAPING FROM HIS HORSE VAL RACES TOWARD THE BEACH, SHEDDING ARMS, ARMOR AND CLOTHING AS HE GOES.

WHENEVER ALETA GOES FOR A SWIM MR. WHISKERS, THE OTTER, WOULD RETRIEVE THE PURLOINED GEM FROM ITS HIDING PLACE, TEASE HER WITH IT, AND SHE WOULD CHASE HIM. OH, WHAT FUN!

THEN THE INTRUDER COMES. HE DOES NOT GLIDE SWIFTLY THROUGH THE WATER LIKE HIS PLAYMATE, BUT SURGES AHEAD USING BIG MUSCLES. MR. WHISKERS DOES NOT LIKE HIM.

HE CHATTERS A BIT AND ROLLS THE PLAYTHING IN HIS PAWS TO ATTRACT HER ATTENTION. NO USE, SHE DOES NOT WANT TO PLAY ANY MORE.... AT LEAST NOT WITH HIM.

HE FOLLOWS THEM UP THE BEACH IN A LAST DESPERATE ATTEMPT TO SAVE HIS FAIR COMPANION FROM A DULL, DRY LIFE, BUT TO NO AVAIL.

© King Features Syndicate, Inc., 1962. World rights reserved. 1325.

SO HE BITES HIS BIG, MUSCULAR RIVAL ON THE LEG AND RETURNS TO THE SEA.

7-1-62

HE TAKES THE GLEAMING TOY TO THE GROTTO WHERE HE KEEPS IT. SOMEHOW IT IS NOT MUCH FUN ANY MORE.

NEXT WEEK- **Farewell and Hello**

Our Story: ONCE AGAIN PRINCE VALIANT RETURNS AND IS QUICKLY REDUCED FROM A FAMED WARRIOR PRINCE TO A PLAIN HUSBAND AND FATHER. BUT HE IS CONTENT.
WHILE SHE BINDS UP HIS BITTEN LEG ALETA EXPLAINS ABOUT HER PLAYMATE AND THE STOLEN JEWEL.

A LONELY FIGURE WATCHES FROM THE BEACH AS THE FLEET SAILS AWAY TAKING HIS PET HUMAN WITH IT.

WOMEN ARE NOTORIOUSLY FICKLE (SO SAY MEN) SO IT IS NO WONDER ALETA FORGETS HER ERSTWHILE PLAYMATE AS SHE WATCHES HER HUSBAND RENEW ACQUAINTANCE WITH HIS CHILDREN AND LISTENS TO ARN'S ACCOUNT OF HIS ADVENTURES.

THE MALE ANIMAL IS NOT TOO DIFFERENT, FOR WHEN HE SEES ANOTHER OTTER SLIDING ON HER BELLY DOWN A CLAY BANK, MR. WHISKERS SQUEALS WITH DELIGHT AND JOINS THE FUN.

THEN HE REMEMBERS THE BRIGHT TOY HE HAD SO MUCH FUN WITH. FROM THE GROTTO WHERE HE HAD HIDDEN IT, HE RETRIEVES ALETA'S JEWEL, WORTH A QUEEN'S RANSOM.

HE GIVES IT TO HIS NEW-FOUND PLAYMATE AND SHE, LIKE ANY OTHER FEMALE, IS DELIGHTED WITH THE SPARKLING BAUBLE ...THEY LIVED HAPPILY EVER AFTER.

AND VAL AND ALETA? WELL, THEY LIVED TOGETHER MUCH AS MARRIED PEOPLE DO EVERYWHERE.

NEXT WEEK — **The Reluctant Nursemaid**

1326.

7-8-62

PRINTED IN BELGIUM BY
proost
INTERNATIONAL BOOK PRODUCTION